How To Pray

Making Real Progress Toward Real Power

Rev. Michael Dorsey

Volume 2 of the How To Live series

This book is part of the How To Live series:

How To Pray
Making Real Progress Toward Real Power
ISBN 978-0-9916205-2-4

Copyright © 2014 by Robert Michael Dorsey

Published by Malakim Press
PO Box 456
Aberdeen, MD 21001

Cover art and design by Rose Watters

Cover photo by Jamal Lawson - http://bit.ly/jlphotography
Back cover photo by Leana Stewart - http://www.smilesfromheavenphotography.com

This book is dedicated to

Reverend Jason P. Evans

a man of prayer I've watched
closely over the years,
and a faithful example
of what it means to
"pray through" to victory
for the glory of God

Acknowledgements

I would like to thank...

My wonderful children, Robbie and Kirsten,
for helping me learn how to pray much more
effectively than I probably otherwise would have!

And my editing team, who all work
very hard to make me look good:

Ted Tansill

George Torbert

Katherine Dorsey

Dan Kurylo

Lisabeth Kurylo

Carolyn Dorsey

Many thanks to you all.

Table of Contents

Foreword

Jesus' disciples watched Him preach, they heard Him teach, they watched Him healing the sick, and they saw when He prayed. They never said to Him, "Lord, teach us to preach," or "Lord, show us how to teach." They never once asked Him, "Lord, teach us how to heal the sick." Not one time.

What they did ask Jesus was this: "Lord, teach us to pray." Why would they ask Jesus that instead of asking Him about all of those other things? The answer is simple: The disciples understood something. Every time Jesus did something amazing, it was preceded by a time of prayer.

They knew that if they could learn to pray the way Jesus' prayed... then they would be able to preach like He preached, and teach like He taught, and heal like He healed. All they had to do was learn how to pray like He did!

Now you can learn it too. This is a How-To book, not a volume of philosophy and theory. Everyone knows they should be praying. That's not the issue. What believers need to understand is how do you do it? In How To Pray you will learn, step-by-step, how to pray following the same prayer pattern Jesus taught His disciples.

It's time to stop analyzing prayer and start taking action. Michael Dorsey will not only help you create your own disciplined prayer life, he also teaches you how to be comfortable in the presence of your Heavenly Father. Prayer time will no longer feel like an obligation or be a source of guilt in your life. Instead it will become a daily appointment you genuinely look forward to.

The last thing in the world the devil wants is for you to learn how to pray. He will try to distract you and keep you from reading this book, but if you will stick with it and actually do what the Word of God says, (be a doer of the Word and not a hearer only), then the days of unfavorable circumstances reigning over your life will be over.

In How To Pray, Michael Dorsey takes a familiar portion of scripture and wrings every ounce of life changing truth out of it! He digs deep into the Lord's Prayer revealing rich spiritual nuggets that will enrich your prayer life. You will be blessed by his transparency and encouraged to pursue a life of prayer.

Kendon Alexander
Senior Pastor
Impact Church, Steubenville OH

"Men may spurn our appeals, reject our message, oppose our arguments, despise our persons, but they are helpless against our prayers."

- J. Sidlow Baxter

"Prayer is not monologue, but dialogue; God's voice is its most essential part. Listening to God's voice is the secret of the assurance that He will listen to mine."

- Andrew Murray

"I used to think the Lord's Prayer was a short prayer; but as I live longer, and see more of life, I begin to believe there is no such thing as getting through it. If a man, in praying that prayer, were to be stopped by every word until he had thoroughly prayed it, it would take him a lifetime."

- Henry Ward Beecher

Introduction

Prayer – the very thought of practicing the art of prayer can be both exciting and intimidating. Exciting because our heart leaps at the very idea of being permitted to conduct conversation with the God of the universe, our Creator and our Savior. Intimidating because we sometimes feel inadequate and ill-prepared when we contemplate engaging in such a task.

All of our lives we're bombarded with everything from books to sermons to New Age teachers, all encouraging us to pray. From the pulpit on Sunday morning to the bumper sticker on the car in front of us in traffic, we're constantly provoked toward prayer. We hear about all the ways prayer could benefit us, yet what all this pressure really accomplishes is to make us more aware of how our own prayer life is falling short of this impossible ideal that's held up before us every day.

No Christian will dispute the importance of prayer. Every believer I've ever met would agree that prayer is one of the most important parts of your Christian life. That being said, there are few Christians who are satisfied with their prayer life, or feel as if they are where they should be in the realm of prayer. Why should this be?

For people who consider themselves to be true seekers, prayer is one of those spiritual topics that captures their attention, whether or not those persons consider themselves to be Christian. Because of the visible collapse of secular humanism's materialistic belief system in our culture, these individuals realize that there's more to life than that which can be seen, felt, measured and quantified. Like the Athenians of Acts 17 worshiping the unknown God, they have great interest in prayer but they know precious little about it.

Many of these "seekers" will eventually make their way to the doors of a church, overcoming their fear of condemnation and distaste of religious hypocrisy, hoping to find something that will be relevant to their lives. They want to better understand how they might be able to commune with the God Who they perceive to be there, because they want to experience Him firsthand. They long to speak with Him, but they don't know how, and no clear instruction ever presents itself.

Others have found salvation through a relationship with the Lord Jesus Christ, but their growth in prayer hasn't progressed much further than their initial experience of prayer when they asked Him to become their Lord and Savior. They would love to draw nearer to Him, to sit at His feet and learn of His wisdom, to obtain answers to needs and to find direction for their lives. Yet they are hindered by their lack of confidence.

Since they've only just begun their Christian walk, they're not sure how to approach their Heavenly Father in prayer. No one has taken the time to teach them how to pray, or helped them get started. Embarrassed by their lack of ability, they never step up to lead prayers themselves, which means they never get to practice, so they never really improve. They believe in the power of prayer and would love to experience it in their own lives, but they don't know how.

Then there are those who have been Christians for most of their lives, the people who have been "in the way" for a while (Acts 9:2). When it comes to prayer, over the years they've heard it all. They are jaded, cynical and hard to impress. They are capable of teaching a lesson from the Bible on prayer, but their deep, dark secret is that prayer still isn't a reality in their own lives.

These are Christians who love the Lord. They want to walk closely with their Heavenly Father. Yet the distractions and disturbances of the day invariably capture their attention, and while caught up in the haste of their daily routine they forget to spend time with the One Who loves them more than any other. When they finally slow down at the end of the evening, they realize another day has slipped away without any prayer taking place. The crushing guilt and condemnation robs them of their peace as they try to lay down and rest, only to repeat the cycle all over again the next day.

If any of these scenarios resemble your spiritual experience, then this book was written for you. Warehouses could be filled with all the books that have been written on prayer. I have read dozens of them myself. Most of these books are good, and some of them are excellent. Why then would I write (and why should you read) yet another book on prayer?

What sets *How To Pray* apart from others before it is that instead of teaching you about prayer, it will teach you how TO pray. You will learn how to make prayer a part of your daily life, for real. When you finish this book, you won't think, "Wouldn't it be wonderful if I could do this?" Instead you'll be thinking, "I can totally do this, and I can't wait to get started!"

You're going to learn how to put your spiritual life in order so that you become disciplined (the root word of disciple) in the practice of prayer. The haphazard prayer life you've had until now will be replaced with consistent, intentional planning sessions with Almighty God, where you'll be able to address any needs that you have and get clear direction from Heaven. You will begin to truly experience real progress toward real power.

Then you will see something amazing start to happen: discipline will turn into desire. Instead of fulfilling a spiritual obligation, prayer will transform into something you want to do, something you look forward to every day. As you embark upon this journey, may God open your heart to fresh revelations from His Word and deposit impartations of divine truth into your spirit, that you may learn *How To Pray*.

Michael Dorsey

July 2014

"God does nothing except in response to believing prayer."

- John Wesley

"We must begin to believe that God, in the mystery of prayer, has entrusted us with a force that can move the Heavenly world, and can bring its power down to earth."

- Andrew Murray

"Prayer is not learned in a classroom but in a closet"

- E.M. Bounds

Chapter 1

The Paradox of Prayer
It's Time To Get Real

"Watch and pray, lest you enter into
temptation. The spirit indeed is willing,
but the flesh is weak."
- Mark 14:38 (NKJ)

Prayer is a Bible subject that "everyone knows about" on the surface, but when you dig a little deeper you quickly realize everyone wishes they knew more about it. Unfortunately, reading books on prayer will help you only so much. It's like taking driver's education classes versus actually driving a car, or taking flying classes versus actually piloting the plane. Prayer is one of those activities that you don't truly begin learning until you actually start doing it.

That's one of the reasons why the enemy works so hard to distract us from prayer. He knows that we have to spend time praying in order to enjoy the benefits of prayer. Therefore, he does everything he can to oppose us. The devil doesn't want us to take advantage of the power that's available to us through prayer. He fills our day with tasks and distractions, exhausting us with busy-ness so we never seem to have the time or energy to pray as we know we should.

Of all of the Christians that I've talked to about prayer over the years, none of them have been fully satisfied with their prayer life. From the brand new believer to the preacher whose ministry is filled with faith and power, everyone recognizes that their prayer life could be better than it is right now.

Ask most Christians, "Is prayer important?" and they will answer, "Yes, of course!" Ask them, "Does prayer make a difference?" and they will almost always say yes. Ask them, "So how much did you pray today?" and they will look away, their voice quieting to a mumbling murmur of excuses as to why they didn't get around to praying today. When it comes to prayer, the Christian ideal and the Christian experience are often very different.

What are we to make of this? Why do we claim to believe that prayer is a valuable activity while not taking full advantage of it? How can we explain this paradox of prayer? To begin with, maybe we need to review some of the benefits of prayer. Perhaps there's not a problem after all. What if we turn the question around and ask why should we pray at all? Why bother in the first place?

The Privilege of Prayer

Imagine you were contacted by the President of the United States, and he requested that you call him every morning so you could talk together for about an hour. For the purposes of this illustration, set aside any political disagreements you may have with the person currently occupying that office, and just consider for a moment what kind of opportunity that would be.

What if the President gave you a special number to call so you could always reach him, and he offered to make the full resources of the Executive Branch of the government of the United States of America available to you whenever you needed them? Not only that, but in addition to requesting a daily appointment with you, he also promised to make himself available to you any time of the day or night.

Does that sound like something that might interest you? Would you look forward to your call each day? Do you think you'd be able to somehow make time for that call with him every morning? Would you be able to come up with any requests that you could bring to him? Or would you have so many requests you'd have to write them all down in a list in order to keep track of them all?

If the phone rang or you received a text or an email while you were on your call with him, do you think you'd be able to stay focused on your conversation with the President? What if a family member came into the room while you were on the call and started talking to you about something? Would you be able to ignore the distraction, or would you allow yourself to be interrupted?

Beyond that, how privileged would it make you feel to know that the President of the United States wanted to spend that time talking to you? What if you were able to get to know him better over time because of your daily calls, and you even became close friends? As you grew closer in your friendship, wouldn't it become even easier to talk to him about the various things you needed, knowing that the President actually cared about you and your situation?

If that sounds like an opportunity you would enjoy, then I have some exciting news for you: you've already been offered something that's even better. The God of Heaven and Earth would like to spend time with you each day, and His Kingdom has way more resources at His disposal than the United States does! It's hard to wrap our minds around that thought, isn't it? How easily we can identify with the Psalmist who said,

When I look at your heavens, the work of your fingers, the moon and the stars, which you have set in place, what is man that you are mindful of him, and the son of man that you care for him? - Psalms 8:3-4

Have you ever paused and taken a moment to consider what a privilege it is to come before the God of the universe, the Creator of Heaven and Earth, to just be able to talk to Him? How amazing is it that Almighty God grants us the honor of coming into His presence at all, much less inviting us to bring our needs and wants to Him in prayer?

Cast your burden on the Lord, and he will sustain you; He will never permit the righteous to be moved. - Psalms 55:22

God knows everything about our lives, yet He seems so incomprehensible to us. We'll never be able to startle

Him or take Him by surprise. He will be fascinating to us for all of eternity, but why does He want to have anything to do with us? How does He not get bored with us? Of course, the answer is He loves us.

> **You number my wanderings;**
> **Put my tears into Your bottle;**
> **Are they not in Your book?**
> **When I cry out to You,**
> **Then my enemies will turn back;**
> **This I know, because God is for me.**
> **- Psalms 56: 8-9 (NKJ)**

Our fellowship with God, through the Lord Jesus Christ, finds its principle expression in our prayer life. It is in our praying that we demonstrate the fact that we actually have a relationship with God; that He speaks with us, and He has entrusted us with this amazing opportunity to speak with Him.

What an honor it is to be permitted to come before the throne of God whenever we want. Why should we pray? Because prayer is an awesome privilege. We need to be aware of this and be mindful that we don't dishonor God by failing to appreciate the privilege of prayer.

The Power of Prayer

Prayer is also a tremendous source of power in our lives. When problems come against us, we can go to God in prayer and access His power to turn those circumstances around. The Bible is full of verses encouraging us to avail ourselves of the power that can be found in prayer. Listen to the words of Jesus:

> **Therefore I say unto you, What things soever ye desire, when ye pray, believe that ye receive them, and ye shall have them. - Mark 11:24 (KJV)**

Notice He didn't say only some things are available. He said, "Whatsoever things you desire." That covers a lot of ground. Then he said if you can simply believe that you receive the answers to your prayers, then you SHALL have them. Not you might have them, unless something goes wrong or you mess up, in which case forget about it. No, He said you shall have whatsoever things you desire.

> **If you abide in me, and my words abide in you, ask whatever you wish, and it will be done for you. - John 15:7**

Ask whatever you wish - and it WILL be done for you. Does it get any better than that? How could Jesus give us such a definitive promise? How could He offer such an iron-clad guarantee? The reason is Jesus understood the power that's available through prayer.

> **Confess your sins to each other and pray for each other so that you may be healed. The earnest prayer of a righteous person has great power and produces wonderful results.
> - James 5:16 (NLT)**

God is still forgiving sins today, He's still in the healing business, and prayers that are brought before Him in the right way still have great power and produce results.

How do you bring prayers to God the right way? That's why you're reading this book.

Let us therefore come boldly to the throne of grace, that we may obtain mercy and find grace to help in time of need. - Hebrews 4:16 (NKJ)

We can come boldly to the throne of God when we need something from Him. We don't need to feel discouraged or intimidated. Obviously we don't want to approach the Lord with a haughty spirit or an arrogant attitude, but we need to understand that we can come to Him whenever we want to, and we can get the answers we require. Truly there is power in prayer.

The Problem of Prayer

If prayer is such a privilege, and if prayer makes so much power available to us, then once again it begs the question, "Why don't we pray more?" It reminds me of a hymn we used to sing in church when I was a young boy:

What a Friend we have in Jesus,
All our sins and griefs to bear?
What a privilege to carry
Everything to God in prayer!

O what peace we often forfeit,
O what needless pain we bear,
All because we do not carry
Everything to God in prayer.

What A Friend We Have In Jesus, by Joseph M. Scriven (1855)

Now I'm not interested in beating you over the head or condemning you over this. Not at all. What *does* interest me is discovering why it's this way. *Why* don't we pray like we know we should pray? The answer is both simple and devastating: we don't believe. We simply don't believe. This unbelief appears in our lives in a number of different ways.

Lack of Confidence

One reason we don't pray like we should is because deep in our heart we think the time we would have spent praying was better used getting ready for the day or scrambling to finish a project before bedtime. If we really believed prayer was worth the investment of time and effort, we would invest the time and effort. We don't because we don't believe. It's just that simple. We lack confidence that prayer would be the best way to make use of that time.

Fear of Boredom

If some of us are truly honest, another reason we don't pray is we're afraid it would be terribly boring. We can barely imagine ourselves spending a whole hour in prayer, much less doing it every day. Yet when we consider the majestic glory of God, how could we possibly be bored in His presence?

This attitude is often caused by exposure to long, stuffy, stodgy prayers made in church, especially at a young age. If that's the mental picture you have of what it means to pray, no wonder you're concerned about being bored! Yet at its root this fear is also a form of unbelief. We don't pray because we don't believe it could be something that's exciting or interesting, much less fun.

Lack of Skill

We also lack faith when we contemplate trying something we don't think we're very good at. No one wants to feel like the slow child in the group. If you're unskillful and inexperienced at prayer, you're probably not going to be very excited about stepping out and trying it, are you? Unfortunately, you can't start where you wish you were. You have to start where you are and move up from there. Often we don't make that effort because we don't believe we know enough about prayer to make the effort worth it.

Too Ashamed

Another reason people don't pray is because they're too embarrassed to come into the presence of God. Maybe they've done something in their past and they can't shake loose of the guilt, or maybe they feel unworthy and undeserving of the goodness of God in their life for whatever reason. I don't care how many mistakes you've made or how bad you think you've been, the power of the Blood of Jesus is greater than any sin you could ever commit.

Failing to come before God in prayer because you're ashamed of something in your life is simply a lack of faith in the power of the Blood of Jesus to pay for your sins. It's unbelief in the finished work of Jesus Christ in His crucifixion, burial and resurrection. You won't ever be able to "come boldly to the throne of grace" (Hebrews 4:16) if you're too ashamed and embarrassed to stand before Him.

All of these reasons come down to the same thing in the end. Why don't we pray like we should? Because we lack faith. There's no need to make it any more complicated than that. We simply don't believe. If we did, we would make prayer the priority in our life that it needs to be.

This is not a new problem. Even Jesus' hand-picked ministry team, the Twelve, made the mistake of not making prayer a priority. At the Last Supper they told Jesus they'd die for Him, but when they tried to pray at Gethsemane they weren't even able to stay awake.

And he came to the disciples and found them sleeping. And he said to Peter, "So, could you not watch with me one hour? Watch and pray that you may not enter into temptation. The spirit indeed is willing, but the flesh is weak."
- Matthew 26:40, 41

All Jesus wanted from them was an hour, yet after all He'd done for them, they weren't able to give Him this short amount of time. Jesus still wants an hour from us today. An hour seems like a long time when we think about praying for an hour, doesn't it? Yet it goes by quickly when it's our favorite prime time TV show. Is praying for one hour really asking too much from us?

Summary

We need to make prayer a priority in our lives. If we could somehow comprehend the awesome privilege of talking to the Creator of Heaven and Earth, and if we could come to recognize the power of prayer - I mean really get hold of it, not just mentally agree with it - then prayer would become more of a priority for us. How can we make that happen?

I know guilt-manipulation won't do it. If that worked, we'd all be prayer experts by now. The only thing that will work is if we make prayer a priority. It's funny how people find the time to do the things that are important to them. Have you noticed that? People will make time for their true priorities.

So the question is, how do we make prayer a priority in our life? How do we overcome our lack of faith, however it manifests in our lives? Whether it's lack of confidence, fear of boredom, lack of skill, or shame and embarrassment, how do we press forward through all of that mess so that prayer can finally become a consistent part of our daily spiritual walk?

Willpower alone won't do it. Good intentions aren't enough either. You're going to need a plan.

Chapter 1 Discussion Questions

1. Is prayer an obligation? Something we are commanded and expected to do? An invitation to share whatever we want? When you think of prayer, what does it look like to you?

2. What makes prayer powerful?

3. When considering the privilege of prayer, how does the illustration of a daily call with the U.S. President help us appreciate the value of prayer?

4. Why does a lack of prayer demonstrate a lack of faith? In what ways could higher faith lead to a deeper prayer life?

5. When considering the problem of prayer, how will studying the scriptures increase our confidence and skillfulness in prayer?

6. When considering the paradox of prayer, what are some of the activities that compete the most with your prayer life? Are they necessary and manageable activities?

7. How can we prevent the necessary, harder-to-manage activities from interrupting our prayer lives?

Chapter 2

The Pattern of Prayer
What's The Plan?

Once Jesus was in a certain place praying. As he finished, one of his disciples came to him and said, "Lord, teach us to pray, just as John taught his disciples." Jesus said, "This is how you should pray..." - Luke 11:1-2 (NLT)

Jesus was a man of prayer. If you're looking for someone to model your prayer life after, no better example can be found than the Lord Jesus Christ. He not only taught about prayer, but He lived what He preached. As we read through the Gospels, it quickly becomes clear to us that prayer was established in the life of Jesus as a holy habit.

And rising very early in the morning, while it was still dark, he departed and went out to a desolate place, and there he prayed. And Simon and those who were with him searched for him, and they found him and said to him, "Everyone is looking for you." And he said to them, "Let us go on to the next towns, that I may preach there also, for that is why I came out."
- Mark 1:35-38

Here at the very beginning of His ministry, we see that prayer was already a part of Jesus' spiritual routine. The night before He had held a very successful healing rally (Mark 1:32-34), but the next day He still got up before sunrise to pray. His disciples sought Him out to let Him know that everyone was looking for Him.

Jesus told them He wasn't going to stay in that place any longer because it was time to move on to other towns instead. How did Jesus decide it was time to move on? He made that decision following a prayer session with His Father. He received His orders from headquarters at the start of the day and moved forward from there.

In these days he went out to the mountain to pray, and all night he continued in prayer to God. And when day came, he called his disciples and chose from them twelve, whom he named apostles: - Luke 6:12-13

It was always through prayer that Jesus received direction for His ministry. Important decisions, like which of His many followers should be included among the Twelve, were made together with the Father in prayer. As His earthly ministry drew to a close, once again we find Him in prayer:

**Then Jesus went with them to a place called Gethsemane, and he said to his disciples, "Sit here, while I go over there and pray."
- Matthew 26:36 (NLT)**

Jesus prayed every single day, starting early in the

morning. He availed Himself of the privilege of prayer and He experienced the power of prayer because He made prayer a priority in His life. We see Him doing this again in Luke 11:1, but this time when He finished one of His disciples approached Him with a request: *"Lord, teach us to pray, as John also taught his disciples."*

Teach Us To Pray

Jesus responded to this unnamed disciple by teaching a pattern of prayer which will also be the plan I'm going to teach you to follow to get your prayer life to the place where you want it to be, but first let's take a moment to notice a couple of things about this particular teaching.

First of all, this lesson on prayer emerged from the context of Jesus' habitual prayer routine. It's doubtful this disciple would've asked Jesus about prayer at all if he didn't often witness Jesus making prayer a priority in His own life. This disciple inquired about prayer because he wanted to make it a priority in his life the same way he saw Jesus doing it. He wanted to follow Jesus' example.

The second thing to take note of is the desire of the disciple. What made him ask Jesus to teach them to pray? This teaching of Jesus in Luke chapter 11 came forth because this disciple pulled it out of Him. As he watched Jesus pray, the man must have seen something that stirred him up on the inside and made him want it too. That same desire is the reason you're reading this book, and it will be a key factor in developing the discipline you're seeking.

The last thing I would like to point out is that this

disciple didn't ask Jesus to teach them *how* to pray. No, instead he said, *"Lord, teach us TO pray."* It doesn't matter if you've read every book ever written on how to drive a car. If you never get in and sit behind the wheel, all of that information will just be a bunch of theories and concepts, with no basis in your real-life experience until you actually start to drive the car. Prayer is the same way. Before you can learn *how* to pray, you first have to learn *to* pray.

This teaching Jesus gave on prayer is commonly referred to as the Lord's Prayer. It appears in Luke 11:2-4 and also Matthew 6:9-13. I will quote these passages in the King James Version first because that's how most of us are used to hearing them:

> **And he said unto them, When ye pray, say, Our Father which art in heaven, Hallowed be thy name. Thy kingdom come. Thy will be done, as in heaven, so in earth. Give us day by day our daily bread. And forgive us our sins; for we also forgive every one that is indebted to us. And lead us not into temptation; but deliver us from evil. - Luke 11:2-4 (KJV)**

In Luke chapter 11, Jesus was speaking to an intimate group of His disciples in a private conversation. Matthew's version is part of the Sermon on the Mount which takes up Matthew chapters 5-7, and it was a teaching given to a great multitude of people. The fact that it appears twice in the Gospels in such different circumstances indicates that Jesus probably gave this teaching on prayer fairly often.

After this manner therefore pray ye: Our Father

which art in heaven, Hallowed be thy name. Thy kingdom come, Thy will be done in earth, as it is in heaven. Give us this day our daily bread. And forgive us our debts, as we forgive our debtors. And lead us not into temptation, but deliver us from evil: For thine is the kingdom, and the power, and the glory, for ever. Amen.
   - Matthew 6:9-13 (KJV)

You might think you're already familiar with the Lord's Prayer. It might seem like old news to you. However, embedded in the Lord's Prayer is the pattern that we can follow to learn to pray, the very same pattern Jesus used to teach His disciples. Going forward, we'll use Matthew's version for this study because it contains a greater amount of detail than the version in Luke's Gospel.

Avoid Vain Repetitions

Jesus cautioned us against praying prayers of vain repetitions. In this context, the word vain means empty or meaningless.

And when you pray, do not use vain repetitions as the heathen do. For they think that they will be heard for their many words. Therefore do not be like them. For your Father knows the things you have need of before you ask Him. In this manner, therefore, pray: Our Father in heaven, Hallowed be Your name." - Matthew 6:7-9 (NKJ)

Notice how right after warning about not praying in vain repetitions, Jesus immediately begins teaching about the Lord's Prayer. Yet how many people today recite that prayer by rote, repeating the words by habit as just another meaningless church tradition?

We aren't supposed to recite the Lord's Prayer word-for-word like an empty religious ritual. Jesus warned against praying with vain repetition. He also told the Pharisees that their religious traditions took all of the power out of God's Word:

"...You nullify the word of God for the sake of your tradition." - Matthew 15:6 (NIV)

We don't want to do that! The fact is we were never meant to simply recite the Lord's Prayer verbatim, over and over, the way it's done today. Jesus said, *"After this manner pray ye..."* (Matthew 6:9), in other words, He was telling them they should "pray along these lines," not that they should "repeat this same exact prayer word-for-word every time they prayed it."

We call this pattern of prayer the "Lord's Prayer" because Jesus is the one who gave it to us, yet it may surprise you to learn Jesus never prayed it for Himself. As the sinless Lamb of God, He never once had to ask, *"...and forgive us our debts, as we forgive our debtors."* (Matthew 6:12) Instead, Jesus told His disciples (and by extension He tells us), *"This is how YOU should pray..."* (Luke 11:2).

In fact, technically this isn't even a prayer for Christians to pray today. The Bible clearly teaches that all New Testament prayer must be made to the Father in the name of Jesus, but the Lord's Prayer doesn't say "in Jesus' name" because Jesus taught it to His disciples before the New Testament era had even begun.

At the Last Supper Jesus told His disciples He would be leaving soon, and the Holy Spirit would be sent in His place. As He was explaining to them what would happen in that soon-coming day, He said:

And IN THAT DAY you will ask Me nothing. Most assuredly, I say to you, whatever you ask the Father in My name He will give you.
- John 16:23 (NKJ)

"In that day" is today! What we call the Lord's Prayer was simply a method or pattern of prayer that Jesus gave His disciples to use during His earthly ministry. After His death and resurrection took place, then the New Testament age would begin and Jesus' followers would start praying to the Father in Jesus' name instead.

We need to be careful that we don't over-emphasize the Lord's Prayer. We shouldn't exalt it to a place of spiritual importance greater than it merits just because it's so familiar and comfortable to us. We also need to take heed of the warning Jesus gave us about falling into the trap of vain religious tradition.

At the same time, it's important that we don't get in the ditch on the other side of the road either, by discounting the Lord's Prayer because we think it's just another tired, old religious tradition. If we do that, we'll miss out on the many revelations contained within it. Jesus' teaching of the Lord's Prayer is the blueprint you can follow to structure your own daily prayer life.

The Plan

So how does this prayer method work? How does following this pattern help you create the consistent prayer life we've been talking about? How does it take the longing you have in your heart to have a real prayer life and turn that desire into the discipline of a praying disciple?

This prayer pattern based on the Lord's Prayer can be divided into six sections. We'll use the King James again, simply because for this passage more people will be familiar with that version:

1) **Position & Promises:** Our Father which art in heaven, Hallowed be thy name.
2) **Priorities:** Thy kingdom come. Thy will be done in earth, as it is in heaven.
3) **Provision:** Give us this day our daily bread.
4) **People:** And forgive us our debts, as we forgive our debtors.
5) **Protection & Power:** And lead us not into temptation, but deliver us from evil:
6) **Praise:** For thine is the kingdom, and the power, and the glory, forever. Amen.

This prayer pattern will become the blueprint for your prayer life. It contains many different types of prayers. You'll be able to learn them all and become quite skillful with them eventually. The Bible talks about many different kinds of prayer. The Apostle Paul frequently taught on this subject. He wrote to the church at Ephesus:

> **Praying at all times in the Spirit, with ALL PRAYER and supplication. To that end keep alert with all perseverance, making supplication for all the saints, - Ephesians 6:18**

The Amplified Bible translates that verse this way: "*...with all manner of prayer...*" There are different kinds of prayer. Paul listed three types of prayer when he wrote to the church at Philippi:

> **Do not be anxious about anything, but in everything by PRAYER and SUPPLICATION with THANKSGIVING let your requests be made known to God. - Philippians 4:6**

In his first letter to his protégé Timothy, Paul also wrote about several different kinds of prayer:

> **First of all, then, I urge that SUPPLICATIONS, PRAYERS, INTERCESSIONS, and THANKS-GIVINGS be made for all people. - I Timothy 2:1**

These verses make it very clear that there are different types of prayer. To say all prayers are the same makes about as much sense as saying all sports are the same. You wouldn't try to hit a home run on a basketball court, nor would you try to score a touchdown at a hockey rink. Each sport has its own rules and conditions that you have to understand and follow. If you don't, you will lose the game and possibly even be disqualified!

Likewise, there are different guidelines for each type of prayer. The rules for the prayer of petition don't apply to the prayer of submission or the prayer of intercession. As we go through the six phases of our prayer blueprint, we will touch on each of these types of prayer as we come to them.

We're going to be focusing on each one of the six sections of this prayer pattern in great detail. By the end of this book, you will learn how to spend just ten minutes praying through each of the six sections listed in the outline above. It's not hard. I'll show you exactly how to do it. Once you know how to do that, you'll be praying an hour a day. Every day!

You won't feel like your prayers are as random as they are now. You'll feel like you're praying with purpose and direction, which will give you confidence and increase your desire to pray even more.

Summary

Jesus was a man of prayer. Every time He received direction for His ministry, it happened during prayer. Prayer wasn't something Jesus turned to as a last resort whenever He got into a jam. In fact, the direction He received in prayer probably helped Him avoid getting into a lot of jams in the first place. Prayer was His lifestyle, and it was also the source of His spiritual power.

The prayer pattern contained within what we today call the Lord's Prayer is something Jesus taught frequently in a variety of different settings. He warned us against praying empty prayers of vain repetition. Instead, He taught that we should use this pattern as a blueprint for prayer the way He intended us to pray.

This plan divides the Lord's Prayer into six sections. By going through these six parts in sequence and spending just ten minutes on each one, you'll be able to pray for an hour or more every day without any problems.

That might sound too good to be true, but I can assure you that if you will make prayer a priority, and if you will commit to learn and follow Jesus' prayer blueprint then you will be amazed at how easy consistent, daily prayer can be.

However, before we start drilling down into these six sections in detail, let us first go over some very practical steps you can take to organize and prepare your personal prayer space.

Chapter 2 Discussion Questions

1. Jesus' disciples never asked, "Lord, teach us to preach," or, "Lord, teach us to heal." Why did they ask Him, "Lord, teach us to pray?"

2. As we consider Jesus' prayer life, what can we learn about the relationship between decision making and prayer?

3. Did Jesus always pray alone? What are the advantages of praying *with* people? What are some possible disadvantages? How do you choose which people you will pray with?

4. Christ's disciples asked him, "teach us to pray" because Jesus made prayer attractive. How can we make prayer attractive to others?

5. Does a committed prayer life bear fruit? If so, what types of fruit will it produce?

6. The word "vain" means: empty, meaningless, and excessively proud. In what ways could a prayer be considered vain? How are our pride and ego associated with vain praying? How can we avoid this?

7. God has patterns throughout all of creation. How can having a pattern for prayer help us focus our prayer life? In what other areas of our lives do we follow a plan to help us succeed?

Chapter 3

Pursuing Prayer

Establishing Your Prayer Life

*Yet the news about him spread all the more,
so that crowds of people came to hear him and
to be healed of their sicknesses. But Jesus often
withdrew to lonely places and prayed.*
- Luke 5:15, 16 (NIV)

Part of the reason that Jesus' prayer life was so consistent is He made the effort to get prayer established in his life. He didn't hope that He'd somehow find the time to pray each day. Instead, He was intentional and purposeful in His approach to prayer. If we're going to be successful in following His example to make prayer a priority, we're going to have to be the same way.

In every supernatural manifestation of God there is both a natural side and a spiritual side. There's a man-ward side and a God-ward side. God will always be faithful to do His part, but we need to make sure that we do our part. For example, consider God's words to Moses at the shore of the Red Sea, with Pharaoh's army in hot pursuit:

The Lord said to Moses, "Why do you cry to me?

> **Tell the people of Israel to go forward. Lift up your staff, and stretch out your hand over the sea and divide it, that the people of Israel may go through the sea on dry ground... Then Moses stretched out his hand over the sea, and the Lord drove the sea back by a strong east wind all night and made the sea dry land, and the waters were divided. - Exodus 14:15-16, 21**

Now we all know perfectly well that Moses stretching out a stick over the water had nothing to do with the Red Sea parting. God is the one who divided the Red Sea. Moses wouldn't have been able to make that miracle happen on his own no matter what he did with that rod. However, what if Moses hadn't obeyed God and stretched forth the rod? Would the sea have still been parted?

You see, even though the miracle wasn't accomplished through Moses' strength, but rather by the power of God alone, the obedience of Moses was required in order for the miracle to happen. This is what the Apostle Paul meant when he described the spiritual gifting of miracles being performed by men of God as the *"working of miracles"* (I Corinthians 12:10).

There is some work that must be done on the man's side. God does the heavy lifting with His power, but man also has his part to play. As Christians, we should strive for excellence in everything we do, serving God to the very best of our ability in every aspect of our life. In this chapter we're going to look at some very practical natural-realm things that you can do to set yourself up for some spectacular sessions of prayer in the spirit realm.

Making Time

The first step to establishing your prayer life is making the time for it. It doesn't really matter whether or not you truly believe you'll be able to pray for an hour each day, if you don't have that spare hour in your schedule to begin with. If you want a consistent prayer life, one in which you really can *"watch with (Him) for one hour"* (Matthew 26:40), then you're going to need to take some time to think about when in your day that hour will actually happen.

The Time Is Already There

The initial reaction many people have is to say, "I just don't have time to pray that long every day." But is that true? The average American watches five hours of TV a day according to the Neilson ratings company. That doesn't even include the time spent surfing the Internet, or checking our social media accounts. The time is there. We just don't manage it very well.

One of the things time management experts recommend to people who want to get a better handle on their time is to keep a log of everything they do for a few days. Almost without fail, people are shocked to learn how much time they waste every day when they see it in black and white. They quickly realize that "I don't have time" is just an excuse.

We have time for just about anything we want to do. However, we don't have time for everything we want to do, which requires us to make choices. That means the real issue is how we will prioritize our time. An hour can't be spent in prayer and spent watching television also. You can't spend the same hour twice. Making time for prayer means identifying the wasteful, low-priority items on your schedule that can be bumped to make room for the much more important activity of prayer.

Your Internal Clock

Another thing to consider when making time for prayer is what type of person you are. Some people are morning persons while others are night owls. I am not a morning person and I don't like coffee so I never drink it. That means it takes me about an hour of being awake before I feel like I'm fully there, but late at night I'm usually awake and alert.

On the other hand, my wife starts to shut down around 10:00 PM and it's just about impossible to hold a conversation with her after 10:30. Yet in the morning she's good to go, which has made for some interesting mornings and evenings over the years, but that's another topic. My point is you have to know what kind of person you are, and what time of day is your "up" time.

And rising very early in the morning, while it was still dark, he departed and went out to a desolate place, and there he prayed. - Mark 1:35

Because Jesus prayed early in the morning, and I'm not a morning person, I would often struggle with feelings of condemnation because I didn't think I was following Jesus' example. I also knew several Christian friends who prayed early in the day, and I would unfavorably compare myself to them. Later I learned the Apostle Paul advised us against allowing those kinds of thoughts into our minds:

For we dare not class ourselves or compare ourselves with those who commend themselves. But they, measuring themselves by themselves, and comparing themselves among themselves, are not wise.
   - II Corinthians 10:12 (NKJ)

I also learned that Jesus didn't pray just early in the morning. He prayed during the day, and He prayed at night too, sometimes praying all night long. So the question isn't what is the best time of day to pray, but what is the best time for *you* to pray?

And after he had dismissed the crowds, he went up on the mountain by himself to pray. When evening came, he was there alone.
   - Matthew 14:23

In spite of the fact that I'm not much of a morning person, God has me praying in the morning right now. There is something about starting the day in the Word and in prayer. It sets the tone for the rest of your day. However, if your experience is different from mine, don't beat yourself up spiritually over it.

You might work at night, or you might have very young children that make your mornings incredibly chaotic and busy as you try to get them ready and out the door to school on time. Identify the rhythms of your body and the flow of your daily schedule, and set your prayer time accordingly.

One thing you'll learn when you decide you're going to serve God is that He may call on you at any time, from the crack of dawn to the midnight hour. Instead of saying, "I'm a morning person," or "I'm a night owl," let your confession be, "I'm God's servant and I'll be whatever He needs me to be." You already know what time of day is your personal prime time, but believe God to help you be available to Him whenever He chooses.

Finally, understand that this extra time for you to pray won't ever just fall into your lap. The devil will see to that. He knows how much stronger you'll get when you start to pray consistently, so he'll do everything in his power to hinder you. Be on the alert and watch out for that. Once you've found the best time for you to talk to God each day, you need to be prepared to guard that time and protect it.

Creating A Place

After you've carved out a time in your schedule when your prayer will happen each day, the next step is to set up the place where you will pray. Obviously as a believer you can pray anywhere at any time, but what I'm referring to is a spot that's been specifically selected and designed by you to be your own personal prayer space.

Sometimes you'll hear Christians use the words "prayer closet" to describe the place where they go to pray. The term refers to a space in their home, perhaps a small room, where they can pray privately and undisturbed – not necessarily a literal closet. So how do you go about creating this space special place where you and God will meet each day?

Remove Any Distractions

The first step is to remove anything from the room that might distract you. It's tough enough to establish a consistent prayer life when you're first starting out. There's no need to make it harder on yourself by trying to pray in unnecessarily challenging conditions.

The room where you'll pray should be made neat and tidy. Don't have things such as mail or school work lying around that you may be tempted to clean up or look at when you're supposed to be praying. If you're praying at your desk, make sure the surface is clear. If your computer is on the desk, you'll want to turn the monitor off and mute the sound.

Other electronics should also be turned off, and your cell phone silenced. You don't want to be just starting to get on a roll praying, only to be interrupted by an incoming text or a status update. All of that can wait until you're finished talking with Him. If we can silence our phone at church and in movie theaters, we can certainly do so during our prayer time. Let all your calls go to voice mail. You're on a more important call right now.

You should also let your family know what you're going to be doing, and that you don't want to be disturbed. I have a room in my basement where I pray, and if I'm in that room and the door is shut everyone knows to leave me alone unless it's something urgent. My kids used to barge in on me when they were younger, but when they got old enough to understand not to interrupt us when we were using the phone, we were also able to teach them not to interrupt us in prayer the same way.

A Quiet Place

In addition to family distractions, you also need to think about your pets. If you can't resist hugging your dog or cat when you're supposed to be praying, you may need to put them out of the room.

On the other hand, if they're just going to bark or meow and scratch at the door for the entire hour while you're trying to pray, you might want to let them in.

Your prayer spot should be a quiet, peaceful place. It should be the kind of room where you can relax and get still before the presence of God, so you can hear Him speaking to your heart.

You should be able to close the door so that you can shut out outside noises. If the walls are too thin, or if you have noisy neighbors stomping around upstairs, you may want to turn on a white noise maker like a SleepMate or a fan.

Another way to block outside noises is with music. A CD player playing soft instrumental music is ideal as long as the music that's playing isn't a distraction to you. You could also use headphones, but if you use your smartphone or iPod be sure to have a playlist ready to go. Otherwise you'll wind up spending a good chunk of your prayer hour fiddling with your .mp3 player.

An Inviting Place

You also want your prayer place to be comfortable and inviting. If all goes according to plan, this is going to be a room where you'll be spending a good deal of time, so you want it to be as pleasant as possible. The temperature should be set so it's just right. The floor should be comfortable to walk on. If it's too cold in the morning, go out and buy a nice rug to put down.

You should also have a comfortable place to sit, but not one that's too comfortable! Nothing is more embarrassing than waking up early in the morning to pray, only to fall asleep again in your big comfy prayer room chair. Ask me how I know.

Another thing you'll want next to your comfortable chair is a small table or similar place where you can put your Bible. You'll probably want to refer to your Bible for certain prayers you'll be praying during your hour, so you want to put it in a place where it's easily accessible.

Lastly, you'll need to have a clock of some kind to track the progress of your prayer hour. As you go through the six parts of the Lord's Prayer pattern, you'll be spending 10 minutes on each section. Many people starting out in this prayer method imagining that it will be difficult to pray on a single section for an entire 10 minutes.

However, once you start to get better at prayer you'll begin to enjoy it, and it's much more likely that it will be the other way around. You'll have to watch the clock to make sure you don't pray for too long on any one part of the prayer! However, if you wind up going over by a couple of minutes on one section or another, you can shave off some time from another section, or you can just go a little longer than the one hour.

Physical Positions In Prayer

Finally, let's address the physical position of your body in prayer. Does it matter? Some people think it does, and they get really hung up about it. Let's take a quick look at what the Bible has to say:

> **Then King David went in and SAT before the Lord and said, "Who am I, O Lord God, and what is my house, that you have brought me thus far?**
> **- II Samuel 7:18**

> **And on the Sabbath day we went outside the gate to the riverside, where we supposed there was a place of prayer, and WE SAT DOWN and spoke to the women who had come together.**
> **- Acts 16:13**

According to these verses, it's fine to sit down when you pray. Other passages refer to kneeling:

> **And he withdrew from them about a stone's throw, and KNELT DOWN and prayed.**
> **- Luke 22:41**

> **When our days there were ended, we departed and went on our journey, and they all, with wives and children, accompanied us until we were**

outside the city. And KNEELING DOWN on the beach, we prayed. - Acts 21:5

You can also pray while standing up:

Then Solomon STOOD before the altar of the Lord in the presence of all the assembly of Israel and spread out his hands toward heaven, and said, "O Lord, God of Israel, there is no God like you, in heaven above or on earth beneath, keeping covenant and showing steadfast love to your servants who walk before you with all their heart; - I Kings 8:22, 23

And whenever you STAND PRAYING, forgive, if you have anything against anyone, so that your Father also who is in heaven may forgive you your trespasses. - Mark 11:25

Or you can pray while lying prostrate before God, flat on your face:

Then Abram FELL ON HIS FACE, and God talked with him, saying: - Genesis 17:3

And going a little farther he FELL ON HIS FACE and prayed, saying, "My Father, if it be possible, let this cup pass from me; nevertheless, not as I will, but as you will." - Matthew 26:39

Do you have to pray with your eyes closed?

WATCH and pray that you may not enter into

temptation. The spirit indeed is willing, but the flesh is weak. - Matthew 26:41

Take heed, WATCH and pray; for you do not know when the time is. - Mark 13:33

Thank God you can pray with your eyes open. Otherwise how would we pray while driving? Ironically, the only physical position of prayer not specifically mentioned in the Bible is the one we hear so often in church: "heads bowed and eyes closed." It really doesn't matter how you position your body when you pray, because prayer is primarily a matter of the heart.

Summary

The fact that you're reading this book tells me two things about you: 1) You have a desire for a more developed prayer life so you can be closer to God, and 2) You have probably tried to establish a prayer habit in your life before and failed, possibly many times. The thought of praying an hour a day may sound like a near-impossible undertaking to you right now.

Maybe you're like me when I first got serious about prayer. I remember the first time I decided I was going to pray for one full hour. I settled on a time when I was going to be home alone so I knew no one would bother me. I picked a room where I could close the door behind me and not be distracted by any outside noises.

I knelt down in front of a comfortable reading chair, the clock hanging on the wall behind me. As I began to talk to my heavenly Father, I really pressed into it. I prayed with earnest determination, and I was grateful to be at a place in my spiritual life where I thought I was finally able to do this – pray for one whole hour.

After some time had gone by, I reached a point where there was a pause in my praying. During that pause I wondered for a moment how much time had gone by. I didn't think it had been an hour yet, but I thought it must be pretty close. I felt like I'd been praying for 45 minutes, at least. Curious to know how long it had really been, I turned to look at the clock behind me. Twelve minutes had passed.

Needless to say I was discouraged, but at the same time it made me angry. I could imagine the devil standing in the corner of the room laughing at me. I have a stubborn streak in me. Stubbornness isn't a bad thing if you learn how to channel it in the proper direction. At that moment I decided that no matter what else happened that day, by God I was going to pray for one whole hour! I was NOT going to allow myself to back off from that commitment.

By the end of the hour I was exhausted. I was able to finish it, but it felt like one of the longest hours I'd ever experienced in my whole entire life. It just seemed to me that after spending time in the presence of God, I should feel energized and inspired, not drained. I felt like there was something I was missing. I wondered what it was.

Just then the Holy Spirit spoke to my heart and said, *"Maybe that's something you could pray about."* I just cracked up laughing. "Very funny, Lord. You're hilarious."

That's something you learn about Him as you get to know Him better. God has a great sense of humor and perfect comedic timing when He decides to use it. Yet hidden in that joke there was a truth I needed to hear and I knew He was right.

As you can see, I haven't always been a superstar prayer warrior, not by any means. The truth is I'm still learning and growing in prayer myself, but I am thankful for where He's brought me thus far. As I pursued my own consistent prayer life, there were two main things I learned that enabled me to start making progress over time.

The first thing was the prayer pattern that Jesus taught His disciples, which we're now ready to start looking at in detail. The second thing was recognizing that even though developing my prayer life seemed like an overwhelming task to me, I didn't have to do it by myself. I had a Partner who would help me.

Chapter 3 Discussion Questions

1. "He (Jesus) was intentional and purposeful in His approach to prayer". What are some essential reasons to be intentional and purposeful about prayer?

2. How is a prayer plan similar to a family budget? Can someone manage to "find" the time to pray in the same way they can always manage to "find" the money for something they really want? Is prayer a "want" or a "need" in your life?

3. Devoting yourself to prayer may require a conversation with your family about private time. How might you begin such a conversation?

4. Good parents help children to build good habits, teaching them to do certain things every day that will lead to a healthy lifestyle. What if a child never brushes her teeth? What if she misses one night? How do good prayer habits lead to a healthy spiritual lifestyle? What are the consequences if you never pray? What if you miss one day?

5. "There's a man-ward side and a God-ward side". What are some things YOU can do to immediately improve your prayer life (the man-ward side i.e. time, location and posture)?

6. What should any initial difficulty in praying for an hour remind us about the God-Ward side of prayer? How can this help prevent guilt if we can't pray for an hour?

Chapter 4

Starting Places
Your Spiritual Position

"After this manner therefore pray ye: Our Father which art in heaven..." - Matthew 6:9 (KJV)

The next two chapters focus on covering the first section of Jesus' teaching on prayer: *Our Father which art in heaven, Hallowed be thy name.* It will take two chapters because there's such an unbelievable amount of material contained within this seemingly short phrase. In fact, these words are really a confession of humility which sets the tone for everything else that will follow.

By starting with the phrase, "Our Father," we immediately set the focus of the prayer session on Him and what He wants, not on ourselves and the things we think we need. Not that you don't come to God with your wants and needs - those will definitely be covered during your prayer hour – but you're making a statement right out of the gate that this prayer session isn't all about you. It's about Him.

The truth that you are not the most important thing in the universe is further emphasized by the pronoun "our" that precedes the word "Father." Jesus didn't teach us to begin the prayer with, "My Father which is in heaven." He

51

taught us to start with "Our Father." This reminds us that we are not alone, but as members of the Church of the Lord Jesus Christ we are part of something greater than ourselves.

We're members in a great body of believers that spans two worlds, covering them both. It's not all about me. It's about God, and it's about my brothers and sisters in Christ all over the Earth. By beginning with those two simple words, "Our Father," you are recognizing God as the center and purpose of your prayer, while simultaneously acknowledging that you are part of a global community of believers and this whole prayer endeavor really isn't about you at all.

Our Father

Notice how this prayer begins with "Our Father" and not "Our Mother." In an earlier time we wouldn't even need to address this point, but today we do. It is Father and not Mother. The various so-called "inclusive language" Bibles that have increasingly appeared over the years begin the prayer, "Our Father-Mother in heaven..." Does it matter how we address God?

The campaign for such inclusive language emerged from a radical feminist argument which asserts that, *"Male domination of society has influenced the way God's character has been understood in the past, and because of that we have not understood the Bible properly due to having viewed it in such a gender-specific fashion. Now that we're learning to study the Bible in new ways and understand the nature of God better, we are not going to be bound by this terrible male-dominated bias."* This is the claim that they make.

While the degree to which our society is actually male-dominated today is a matter of great debate, the Bible is absolutely clear in its declaration of God's fatherhood. It is unequivocally clear. This is an important issue which does concern you, because one of the main ways the cause of the Gospel is being fought against today is in the arena of gender and sexuality, especially within the framework of the church.

What should our answer be to those who say, "Well, I don't like to pray Our Father who art in heaven. I want to pray, 'Our mother who art in heaven, hallowed be your name?'" I would say, first of all, when we view the Bible with humility and with honesty, it is impossible for us to evade the fact that the Bible always uses "Father" as the designation of the first person of the Trinity.

We dare not tamper with God's self-revelation in order to appease the demands of contemporary society, especially since these demands are emerging in large measure from those who do not even accept the Bible's authority or its inspiration. God makes it very clear throughout the Bible that we are not to tamper with His written Word:

You shall not add to the word that I command you, nor take from it, that you may keep the commandments of the Lord your God that I command you. - Deuteronomy 4:2

> **Every word of God proves true; he is a shield to those who take refuge in him. Do not add to his words, lest he rebuke you and you be found a liar.** - Proverbs 30:5, 6

Secondly, we do need to acknowledge and recognize that God sometimes uses the picture of motherhood when relating to His people.

> **As one whom his mother comforts, so I will comfort you; you shall be comforted in Jerusalem.** - Isaiah 66:13

However, just because God tells us He will sometimes act in the way a mother would act, that doesn't change the fact that He's our Father. We acknowledge that God sometimes uses the picture of motherhood when relating to His people. Yet the Lord Jesus made it plain that it was the Father that He came to reveal to us.

> **All things have been handed over to me by my Father, and no one knows the Son except the Father, and no one knows the Father except the Son and anyone to whom the Son chooses to reveal him.** - Matthew 11:27

We've already mentioned how Jesus taught that all New Testament prayer is to the Father, in His name:

> **And in that day you will ask Me nothing. Most assuredly, I say to you, whatever you ask the Father in My name He will give you.** - John 16:23 (NKJ)

The desire to change this profound illustration of God's relationship to His people emerges either from a failure to understand the perfection of God's revelation in scripture, or from an unhealthy preoccupation with gender issues, where people perceive threats to women everywhere, even when the threat really isn't there.

We do not call God "Father" because we view Him through a prism of male domination. It is simply a result of the fact that God, in the way that He has chosen to disclose Himself to us, has revealed Himself as Father, Son and Holy Spirit. This is not in any way denigrating toward women or the feminine virtues, despite the fact that some have claimed otherwise.

A Good Father

We understand, based on the way God has chosen to reveal Himself to us in Scripture, that God is our Father, but what kind of Father is He? Sadly, there are people to whom the illustration of God as Father is not a great comfort. Many have been the victims of dads who were tyrants and ruled over their lives like dictators. Some have even had fathers who were abusive, who were users, or who molested them. Others were abandoned by fathers they never knew because the fathers vanished from their lives when the children were very young.

If the heavenly Father is anything like those earthly fathers, then why would we ever want to know Him? However, we all have some understanding of the ideal of fatherhood. You recognize in some measure what a father is supposed to be, even if your own father completely dropped the ball and failed to meet those expectations.

God is not just like a father. He is Father. He is the Father. The Bible reveals God to be the model of fatherhood against which all other fathers are measured. If you want to know what a true father is supposed to look like, don't look at your earthly father or any other father you know, no matter how good he may appear to be.

Instead, open the pages of the Bible and see the heart of the Father revealed in the nature of God, the One who is: loving, faithful, true, just, merciful, patient, kind, slow to anger, affectionate, providing, and wise. He is the model Father. In Matthew 23:9, Jesus says:

And call no man your father on earth, for you have one Father, who is in heaven.
   - Matthew 23:9

This is a strange verse that puzzled me for a long time. What does it mean? Is Jesus saying I should be calling my own dad by his first name instead of calling him father? No, not at all. Jesus is speaking here in an ultimate or absolute sense. In the next verse He says:

Neither be called instructors, for you have one instructor, the Christ. - Matthew 23:10

He said not to call any man "teacher" because Christ is our Teacher. Yet we know from other passages of Scripture that God has placed anointed teachers in the church, and we are instructed to receive them. Failing to do so would be a mistake and a sign of spiritual immaturity.

So what is Jesus saying here?

Jesus is teaching us that we are not to look to any man as our ultimate instructor, because that place belongs to Jesus Christ alone. Men will sometimes make mistakes. Sometimes they will fail us. Therefore, all teachers are to be evaluated according to the standard set by the Great Teacher. What they say must be compared with what He said. If they conform to His example then we may choose to follow them. If they do not, then they must be rejected.

Jesus talks about fathers in the same way. You shouldn't call any man "Father" in an ultimate sense, because only God is the standard by which we judge fatherhood. The godliest father on earth is but a shadow of His perfection. God is the model Father, and we see this throughout the entire Bible.

In the Old Testament, God models Fatherhood in His relationship to the nation of Israel. In the Gospels, God models Fatherhood in His relationship to Jesus Christ, His Son. In the New Testament, God models Fatherhood in His relationship to the Church. This leads us to the final question about the Fatherhood of God.

Is He Your Father?

Here is a question of absolutely critical importance. Is He your Father? Before you can refer to God as "Father" He has to first become your Father. This is an issue that has been complicated by man's ideas and confused by man-made religious tradition. Many people assume that God is everyone's Father, but He is not. Jesus told the Pharisees:

You are of your father the devil, and your will is to do your father's desires. He was a murderer from the beginning, and does not stand in the truth, because there is no truth in him. When he lies, he speaks out of his own character, for he is a liar and the father of lies. - John 8:44

Spiritually speaking, God can be your Father, but if He isn't, then your father is the devil according to Jesus. People get hung up on what religion you follow or what denomination you're a part of, but it's really not about that. The issue is what spiritual family are you a member of? You're either in one or the other. How can you know for sure that God is your spiritual Father?

When you go before Him in prayer, what gives you this access to God the Father? What gives you the right to approach Him in prayer at all? The answer is the Blood of Jesus Christ that was shed for you. The apostle John wrote:

And the Word was made flesh, and dwelt among us, (and we beheld his glory, the glory as of the only begotten of the Father,) full of grace and truth. - John 1:14

Jesus was the only begotten of the Father. Yet after His resurrection, He's called the "firstborn" from the dead:

**And he is the head of the body, the church: who is the beginning, the firstborn from the dead; that in all things he might have the preeminence.
- Colossians 1:18**

If there's a "firstborn" that means there must be a "second born" and a "third born" and so on. When you were "born again" (John 3:3) your number got added to the list in there somewhere!

Let us therefore come boldly unto the throne of grace, that we may obtain mercy, and find grace to help in time of need. - Hebrews 4:16 (KJV)

How humbling it is to be able to enter into conversation with the Creator of the universe, knowing that the only reason we're able to do so is because of the shed Blood of Jesus Christ. Because of what Jesus did in His death, burial and resurrection, we have been adopted into the Father's family.

**He predestined us for adoption as sons through Jesus Christ, according to the purpose of his will.
- Ephesians 1:5**

That means we are now members of God's family, and we are as much the son or daughter of God as Jesus Himself. That's hard to wrap your mind around sometimes, but the Bible makes it clear.

**To redeem those who were under the law, so that we might receive adoption as sons.
- Galatians 4:5**

If you haven't been adopted into God's family yet, that's easy to fix. God has already done all the work for you through the finished work of Jesus Christ, and you can become a member of the Father's family right now. Stop reading here and go to page 185. Ask Jesus Christ into your heart to be the Lord of your life, and then you'll be able to truly pray, "Our Father..."

For you did not receive the spirit of slavery to fall back into fear, but you have received the Spirit of adoption as sons, by whom we cry, "Abba! Father!" - Romans 8:15

The word *Abba* here isn't referring to a disco band from Sweden. *Abba* is a Greek word that has no direct English equivalent, so the translators just copied it directly into our English Bible. It's a word that speaks of intimacy and comfortable familiarity. The closest word we have in the English language to *Abba* would be "Daddy."

When you come into God's presence, you can begin by praising Him for sending Jesus to die for your sins, and then thank Him for raising Jesus from the dead, that you might also be able to enjoy the benefits of eternal life and have access to speak to God the Father whenever you need to. Praise God!

Which Art In Heaven

As you begin your prayer hour, you also need to take a moment to recognize where God is. He is *"our Father which art in Heaven"* (Matthew 6:9 KJV). From His heavenly perspective, God sees everything.

I the Lord search the heart and test the mind, to give every man according to his ways, according to the fruit of his deeds. - Jeremiah 17:10

And no creature is hidden from his sight, but all are naked and exposed to the eyes of him to whom we must give account. - Hebrews 4:13

This speaks of His position over us, not just in divine power, but also in divine perspective. He is not limited by the earthly viewpoint through which you and I see things. He knows the end from the beginning. He sees things and knows things that you don't. When you pray "Our Father which art in Heaven," you are acknowledging that truth.

For now we see through a glass, darkly; but then face to face: now I know in part; but then shall I know even as also I am known.
- I Corinthians 13:12

Our own perspective is so much more limited. We can't see all of the things that God can see. We don't know what the future is going to bring. We can't see into the hearts of the people around us, to know what they're really thinking and what their true intentions are. Solomon, the wisest King Israel ever had, gave this counsel:

Be not rash with your mouth, nor let your heart be hasty to utter a word before God, for God is in heaven and you are on earth. Therefore let your words be few. - Ecclesiastes 5:2

Recognizing where God sits, in Heaven, relative to our own position on the earth, will help us to choose our words more wisely when we pray. This can also be a source of great spiritual peace for us. I know I can relax when I'm talking to God. I don't have to have everything all figured out in advance, because He already does. I don't have to see the whole picture right now, because He already does.

I just need to spend time in His presence gleaning from Him the things that He knows which I haven't seen yet. I can gain His perspective, and that will enable me to make more informed decisions about the choices that are before me each day, something I wouldn't be able to do if I was limited to just my own scope of vision. What a blessing it is to be able to take advantage of His infinite and eternal perspective.

Summary

A lot of people have what our culture calls "Daddy issues." The problems and misconceptions resulting from the hurts and wounds caused by poorly skilled fathers can corrupt our impression of God the Father and sabotage our attempts at prayer right from the very beginning. You aren't ready to even get started in prayer until you first understand your own spiritual position as a child of your heavenly Father, and that He is a good Father.

When my children want something, they have no hesitation about approaching me for it. I may be working on a project in the house, or deep in concentration studying the Word, or lost in a good book, or talking to my wife about things that are coming up, or catching up with a good friend at church. It doesn't matter. They don't care. They'll walk right up to me and say, "Daddy."

If I don't look up at them right away they'll say it

again: "Hey Dad." If I still don't immediately acknowledge them, they'll say it again, a little louder this time. "Daddy!" They don't come into my presence walking on eggshells, with great fear and trepidation. They just walk right up to me so they can make their desires known.

They don't have any fear because they know I'm their father and I love them. I've proven my character to them over the years and they know they can trust me, so they are very comfortable and relaxed when they come before me.

While I try to be a good father, God *is* a good Father. His love for us gives us the courage to approach Him, and His unchanging character gives us the confidence to call on His name.

Chapter 4 Discussion Questions

1. How should the revelation of God as "Our Father" affect our approach to God in prayer? Why does it matter?

2. Why is it important for us to address God using the terminology He has chosen to use to reveal Himself in the holy scriptures?

3. Why is it necessary to overcome gender issues, life experiences, and religious traditions when relating to God as "our Father?"

4. How can a greater understanding of God as "our Father" improve both the quality and quantity of prayer in our lives?

5. In popular media the television Dad is often the fall guy – the clueless one or the dreamer who can never deliver. Can you think of any positive role models for fatherhood in your life? Why has the enemy, through the media, attacked the image of fatherhood?

6. In what ways is it helpful to acknowledge God's position in Heaven vs. our position upon the Earth? How does doing so at the start of Jesus' prayer pattern help set the tone for the rest of the prayer that follows?

Chapter 5

Personal Prayer
Working With Your Covenant Partner

He sent redemption to his people;
He has commanded his covenant forever.
Holy and awesome is his name!
- Psalms 111:9

Who is this Father that's in Heaven, anyway? It's not enough to know that He's the Creator and King of all creation. That's what He is, not who He is. When you pray, you aren't praying to an abstract, impersonal force. You're praying to a Person, the Father. You need to know Him, not just know about Him.

Did you know that all faith must ultimately be placed in a person? If I tell my daughter that I'll pick her up at 5:00, she has faith in that statement based on her knowledge of me as a person, because she knows from past experience that she can rely on me.

If I have faith that a chair will hold my weight when I sit down in it, my faith is actually in the original builder of the chair, that he was skillful enough to know what he was doing when he made it.

In the same way, our spiritual faith is based on a Person. Many claim to have faith in God's Word, and that's a good thing, but faith in someone's word can only be based on the character of the person who spoke that word.

In Father God's case, we know that He, as a Person, is faithful, and so we are able to put our faith in His Word, knowing that He'll be faithful to what He has spoken. We trust in His Word because we trust the character of the One who spoke the Word.

A personal relationship with God and a good understanding of His character are the foundation of your prayer life. That's because when you're praying, it's not something that you're doing by yourself. Even if you're home alone praying in your secret place, you're still not by yourself. Your heavenly Father is your spiritual Partner in prayer.

Prayer isn't something you do for Him. Rather, it's something you do with Him, together. If you think prayer is an activity you perform all by yourself, your thinking is wrong. At the same time, if you think you're just going to bring God a wish list without putting forth any effort on your part, that's also incorrect.

Likewise the Spirit HELPS us in our weakness. For we do not know what to pray for as we ought, but the Spirit himself intercedes for us with groanings too deep for words. - Romans 8:26

In the opening part of this verse, the word "helps" is *sunantilambanomai* in the original Greek text. It literally translates as "to take hold together against". The word "together" implies that your participation is required. The Holy Spirit takes hold together with you against the problem. If you just sit back and don't ever take hold of the problem, the Holy Spirit has nothing to "take hold of" with you.

But thanks be to God, when you do go to pray about something, you're not doing it all by yourself. You're not left to pray on your own. Knowing that the Holy Spirit will help you in prayer lets you approach the Father with a degree of boldness that you might not have otherwise. At the same time, it helps you cultivate a spirit of humility as you recognize that you wouldn't be able to pray effectively if you were on your own.

Since your daily hour of prayer will be spent with this Person, it would probably be a good idea to learn some more about Him. You wouldn't go into business with a partner you didn't know anything about, would you? You probably wouldn't even agree to take part in a new project unless you knew at least one other person involved. So then why would you try to work on things in your life, things that have eternal implications, without getting to know your spiritual Partner?

Hallowed

After, *"Our Father who art in heaven,"* the next part of the prayer pattern is *"Hallowed be thy name."* What does that phrase mean? To hallow something means to sanctify it or to make it holy. You might be thinking, "Okay, great. Now what does that mean?"

To sanctify a thing means to set it apart as holy unto God. For example, when you get your paycheck, you should set aside 10% as a tithe that you dedicate and give back to God. When you do so, the tithe becomes holy. It is now set apart for Him (Leviticus 27:30). It's no longer considered common like the other 90% of your money. It has been hallowed.

So then what does it mean to hallow God's name? How do we set apart God's name as holy? How do we not treat the name of God as though it were a common thing? One way we hallow God's name is by honoring the third commandment:

You shall not take the name of the Lord your God in vain, for the Lord will not hold him guiltless who takes his name in vain. - Exodus 20:7

Many take this verse to mean that we should not use the Heavenly Father's name together with profanity or a curse word. Others believe that taking His name with our lips while living a life of sin is taking His name in vain. While both of these could be true, let's take a look at the dictionary's definition of the word "vain":

1. Having no real substance, value, or importance; empty; void; worthless; unsatisfying.
2. Destitute of force or efficacy; effecting no purpose; fruitless; ineffectual; as, vain toil; a vain attempt.

From these definitions we learn that taking God's name in vain means taking it for an empty or worthless purpose, or using His name in a way that won't accomplish anything. While this could certainly include profanity, it isn't limited to that alone. This coming Sunday many churches will be filled with people taking God's name in vain. Does that shock you?

How many people do you know who claim to be Christians, yet they're just going through the motions of religious tradition? When they mouth God's name, it isn't for any specific purpose or reason. They aren't saying His name with the intention of accomplishing anything. They aren't expecting anything to happen. Their words are empty.

Whenever you spend any time in prayer, always do it with intention. Have a purpose. Pray with expectation, with the hope that the thing you're praying about will come to pass. Don't pray empty prayers. Never call on His name without a reason.

Another way to dishonor His name is to be disobedient in the manner we use it. For example, we've already read where Jesus told His disciples that when the New Covenant began we would pray to the Father in the name of Jesus. That's the way our Lord said we should do it.

Yet many Christians end their prayers with, "We pray for Jesus' sake. Amen." First of all, there's not one scripture in the entire Bible that directs us to pray for Jesus' sake. That's a tradition of dead religion that Satan has tried to insert into the church to deprive us of the power that resides in Jesus' name:

And HIS NAME, through faith in His name,

HAS MADE THIS MAN STRONG, whom you see and know. Yes, the faith which comes through Him has given him this perfect soundness in the presence of you all. - Acts 3:16 (NKJ)

On top of that, it's a lie anyway. You aren't praying for Jesus' sake. He doesn't need your prayers. You're praying for your sake! Why not just be honest about it and keep yourself in obedience to the Word? We hallow His name when we use it as He instructed us.

Finally, we can also hallow God's name through praise. When we enter into a session of prayer we should always begin by remembering Who it is that we are talking to. We should recognize what His position is, and then we should spend some time hallowing His name in praise. This leads to the next very important question: What is God's name, anyway?

What's in a Name?

Before we can hallow God's name we have to understand what His name is. What is God's name? Is it Melvin? How about Biff? Maybe Herman? I'm not being irreverent here. I'm intentionally jogging your mind out of the rut of traditional religious thinking right now. What is God's name?

First of all, God's name isn't God. God is a title, like President is a title. We refer to President Bush or President Obama, but President isn't the actual name. Their names are George Bush and Barack Obama. They can and should be addressed by their title, Mr. President, but that is not either one of their names. Likewise you can address your heavenly Father as "God," but you need to understand that's His title, not His name. So again I ask, what is God's name?

In reality, no name could ever hope to cover the fullness that is God. He is so big and so infinite that we can never hope to understand Him on our own, with our limited, finite minds. God understands this, so He has given us many different names that we may call Him, and in each of those names He has revealed something of Himself to us so we can understand Him better.

Your name equals your reputation. If you have a good name in town, that means you have a good reputation. Likewise, it's very easy for a bad reputation to get attached to your name. It takes many good deeds to build a good reputation, and only one bad one to lose it. That may seem unfair, but that's still how it is.

A brand for a company is like a reputation for a person. A company earns a good reputation by trying hard to do things well, yet one major problem can become a public relations disaster that turns that company's brand from a household standard into a running joke.

If you have a good name, it can help you get things accomplished. For example, say you and I had talked and you agreed to let me borrow something from you. I might ask my brother to come by and pick it up, but if you didn't know who he was you might ask, "Why should I give this to you?" But if he told you, "I'm Michael Dorsey's brother," then you'd probably give it to him, all because of my name.

I try really hard to maintain my good name. I want my name to become a legacy that I can hand down to my children, something that will help to make their lives easier than mine has been – not that mine has been bad, but I want theirs to be even better. However, no matter how good my name becomes, it will never be anywhere close to how good God's name is.

I will worship toward Your holy temple,
And praise Your name
For Your lovingkindness and Your truth;
For You have magnified Your word above all
Your name. - Psalms 138:2 (NKJ)

The only thing that is higher than the Name of God is the written Word of God. God has magnified His Word even above His name.

If someone claims to be doing something in God's name, but it doesn't line up with the Word, then you know that person is practicing error. Even when they try to attach credibility to what they're saying by telling you, "This came from God," the Word of God always takes precedence over anyone's teachings or supposed spiritual experiences.

No one has a greater reputation than God. There is no one Who is wiser, more caring, or more faithful to His Word than He is, and His perfect reputation is yet another reason why His name is set apart as holy. With all of that understanding, we can now return to the question what is God's name?

Jehovah

God has many names. He intentionally uses His names as a way to reveal Himself to us, and also to teach us about His reputation. Since He is infinite and all-encompassing, one name isn't sufficient to accomplish this. God revealed one of His names when He was calling Moses from the burning bush:

Then Moses said to God, "Indeed, when I come to the children of Israel and say to them, 'The God of your fathers has sent me to you,' and they say to me, 'What is His name?' what shall I say to them?" And God said to Moses, "I AM WHO I AM." And He said, "Thus you shall say to the children of Israel,' I AM has sent me to you.'
- Exodus 3:13-14 (NKJ)

This is an English translation of the name *Jehovah*. God said "I AM," which is the verb of being. He's telling us here that He's not just the God of some distant hoped-for future, but He's the God of right now.

When He tells Moses, "I AM WHO I AM," He's saying He won't change. In effect God is stating, "I'll be that right-now God whenever You need Me. I'll be what you need Me to be when you need Me to be that." I really like the way the Amplified Bible renders this verse:

And God said to Moses, I AM WHO I AM and WHAT I AM, and I WILL BE WHAT I WILL BE; and He said, You shall say this to the Israelites: I AM has sent me to you! - Exodus 3:14 (AMP)

God revealed Himself as Jehovah when he told Moses, *"I AM THAT I AM"* (Exodus 3:14). The words "I AM" indicate He is that right now, and by repeating "that I AM," God is saying He will always be that. He won't change.

For I am the Lord (JEHOVAH), I do not change; Therefore you are not consumed, O sons of Jacob. - Malachi 3:6 (NKJ)

So Jehovah God says, "I AM." This causes me to wonder, "God, you are... what?"

The Redemptive Names of God

In seeking an answer to the question, "What is God's name?" we have introduced the name of Jehovah. This name is always associated with the plan of redemption, a theological term that simply means all the things that Christ achieved for us on the cross and in His resurrection. (You'll always find that everything ultimately comes back to the Lord Jesus Christ.)

Salvation includes so much more than the new birth and going to Heaven when you die. The word translated "salvation" in our Bible is the Greek word soterion, which includes salvation, healing, blessing, protection, and more. Just as God reveals His character and His nature to us through His names, in like manner He also uses names that reveal to us the various facets of His redemptive work in our lives.

There are several major redemptive names of God given in the Bible. We're going to look at nine of them that God uses to reveal Himself to us as our Savior in nine different areas of our lives. These are compound names that start with Jehovah, followed by the second part of the redemptive name. Let's look at each of these redemptive names and see what they reveal to us.

Jehovah-Tsidkenu (SID-ken-oo)
The Lord my Righteousness

We can stand before the throne of God without any shame or fear, not because of our own righteousness, but only because of the righteousness of the Lord Jesus Christ, which is credited to us when we accept His sacrifice for our sins by faith.

In those days Judah will be saved, and Jerusalem will dwell securely. And this is the name by which it will be called: 'The Lord is our righteousness *(Jehovah-Tsidkenu)*.'
- Jeremiah 33:16

There's both a "right-now" and a "not-yet" side of redemption. While we can enjoy the many benefits of our salvation today, these blessings are but a down payment on the fullness of the glory of our inheritance in Christ Jesus. We can praise *Jehovah-Tsidkenu* not only for giving us right-standing with Him today, but also looking ahead to the righteousness that will be ours in the world to come.

Jehovah-Shalom (sha-LOME)
The Lord my Peace

Peace, or shalom, appears over 400 times in scripture.

As a redemptive name of God, *Jehovah-Shalom* first appears in the Book of Judges, where God told Gideon not to be afraid when He appeared to him:

But the Lord said to him, "Peace be to you. Do not fear; you shall not die." Then Gideon built an altar there to the Lord and called it, The Lord Is Peace (Jehovah-Shalom). To this day it still stands at Ophrah, which belongs to the Abiezrites. - Judges 6:23, 24

Often translated as welfare, good health, prosperity, favor, and rest, the peace of God is one of the most precious and valuable benefits of being a child of God. It represents wholeness, contentment, and satisfaction as we live our lives in harmony with God's will. He is our peace.

Jehovah-Rapha (RA-fa)
The Lord my Healer

The benefits of our redemption are not limited to spiritual issues alone. They also cover the healing of our physical body. God revealed Himself as *Jehovah-Rapha* to Moses and the children of Israel at the waters of Marah.

"If you will diligently listen to the voice of the Lord your God, and do that which is right in his eyes, and give ear to his commandments and keep all his statutes, I will put none of the diseases on you that I put on the Egyptians, for I am the Lord, your healer (Jehovah-Rapha)."
- Exodus 15:26

The day will come, in the resurrection, when we will be given glorified bodies that never grow weary or diseased, but in the meantime we can believe God for healing in the body we have now. Just as He turned the bitter water of Marah sweet, so will He take our broken bodies and make them healthy and strong.

Jehovah-Jireh (YIR-ay)
The Lord my Provider

This name of the Lord literally translates to "the Lord who sees." It was first revealed on Mount Moriah where God made provision of a substitute sacrifice instead of the son Abraham was willingly prepared to offer.

So Abraham called the name of that place, "The Lord will provide *(Jehovah-Jireh)*"; as it is said to this day, "On the mount of the Lord it shall be provided *(Jehovah-Jireh)*." - Genesis 22:14

Jehovah-Jireh literally translates to "the God Who sees." The Bible says God knows the end from the beginning (Isaiah 46:10).

With his ability to see ahead, God was able to make provision (pro + vision) for Abraham by making sure ahead of time that the ram he would need would be there. Jehovah-Jireh is also able to look ahead in our lives, to make sure we will always have what we need.

The location of this miracle is important because it's the first recorded instance in scripture of the naming of a place after a divine intervention.

Jehovah-Sabaoth (SAB-ee-oth)
The Lord of Hosts

This name comes from the Hebrew word *Sabaoth*, meaning hosts, and is related to the military functions of warfare and service. A more contemporary rendering of this poetic term would be "Lord of Armies." This name appears in the Bible at a time when Israel was struggling to secure the Promised Land from its enemies.

> **Now this man used to go up year by year from his city to worship and to sacrifice to the Lord of hosts (Jehovah-Sabaoth) at Shiloh...**
> **- I Samuel 1:3**

This name appears 14 times in the Book of Haggai and is mentioned 24 times in Malachi. The Prophet Zechariah uses *Jehovah-Sabaoth* an amazing 53 times in his writings, which focus on God's actions in judgment and blessing upon His people. The Lord is mighty in battle, and He is our champion. We can rely on the faithful protection He and His armies of angels provide.

Jehovah-Nissi (NEE-see)
The Lord my Banner

Soon after escaping the Egyptians at the Red Sea, Moses found himself standing on a hillside as the Israelites battled the Amalekites in the valley below. As long as he held his hands in the air, Israel would be winning, but as soon as his hands were lowered, they would start losing. When his hands grew too tired to hold up any longer, Aaron and Hur helped hold them up until the battle was won.

> **And Moses built an altar and called the name of
> it, The Lord Is My Banner *(Jehovah-Nissi).*
> - Exodus 17:15**

Moses took care that God alone would get the glory for their victory over Amalek. Instead of taking credit himself, or giving credit to General Joshua, he built an altar to God's honor. Moses recognized that it was the presence and power of *Jehovah-Nissi* which was the banner under which they served, and the banner by which they were unified. We must also remember to give God the glory for the victories He brings in our lives.

Jehovah-M'Kaddesh (em-CAD-esh)
The Lord Who Sanctifies

Our word "holiness" is from the Hebrew word *Kaddesh* and is related to the word "sanctify." It's translated in various passages as dedicate, consecrate, hallow, and holy. Sanctification is necessary for service.

> **You are to speak to the people of Israel and say,
> 'Above all you shall keep my Sabbaths, for this
> is a sign between me and you throughout your
> generations, that you may know that I, the Lord,
> sanctify you *(Jehovah-M'Kaddesh).* - Exodus 31:13**

After battle the soldiers of Israel were required to remain outside the camp for seven days so they could sanctify themselves (Numbers 31:19). It's important that we as Christians also take time to sanctify ourselves every time we're forced to do battle with the evil in this world.

Jehovah-Shammah (SHA-mah)
The Lord Who Is There

God gave the Prophet Ezekiel a vision of His heavenly city. Among other things, Ezekiel noted:

The circumference of the city shall be 18,000 cubits. And the name of the city from that time on shall be, The Lord Is There *(Jehovah-Shammah)*." – Ezekiel 48:35

When Jesus was giving His parting instructions to His disciples at the Last Supper, He told them that He was leaving them soon, but in His place the Holy Spirit would come. He said the Holy Spirit would abide with us forever (John 14:16). We can take great comfort in the presence of God. Just knowing He is there can be a great source of peace and encouragement for us.

Jehovah-Rohi (RO-hee)
The Lord my Shepherd

The 23rd Psalm starts off with these beautiful words:

The Lord is my shepherd *(Jehovah-Rohi)*; I shall not want. - Psalms 23:1

Like Israel, we as Christians must learn to appreciate the Lord of righteousness, peace, healing, provision, protection, glory, sanctification and faithful presence of our God as we continue to allow Him to shepherd us on our journey.

Yet we are still spiritual pilgrims. This world is not our home, we're just passing through. Our wilderness journey, with all of its weariness, physical needs, duties, dangers, and difficulties reminds us of our continuous need for *Jehovah-Rohi,* the Shepherd whose love, care and resources we can rely on as we walk the unknown paths that lie before us.

There are many other names God has given us to that reveal His nature besides these nine redemptive names, such as *Elohim, El Elyon, El Shaddai,* and *Adonai.* I encourage you to study the names of God further so you can include even more of them in your prayer.

The truth of the matter is we could probably fill an entire book teaching on any one of these redemptive names, but this is enough to get you started. The point of focusing on the redemptive names of God is that each one points to a key benefit that we received when we were redeemed from the kingdom of darkness and translated to the kingdom of His dear Son, over 2,000 years ago.

Summary

For the last two chapters we've been talking about the first part of the prayer outline that Jesus gave His disciples. We traditionally refer to it as the Lord's Prayer. However, it's actually a prayer blueprint that you can learn and follow in order to help you develop your own disciplined daily prayer life. I'm not talking theory here.

I'm talking about your getting to a place where you're praying up to an hour a day, and it's not a struggle and it isn't boring.

Imagine coming into the presence of God to open a time of prayer, not awkwardly trying to figure out what to do first, but knowing exactly how you plan to begin and what you want to say. Think of the confidence you'll have. Imagine the sense of purpose you'll feel. Whereas before you would secretly dread approaching your prayer appointments, now your new confidence and sense of purpose will motivate you to want to pray. You'll actually start looking forward to your next prayer session.

How does it work? Well, so far we've covered only section one: *"Our Father, which art in Heaven, hallowed be Thy name."* Following the outline provided for you in Appendix A (page 173), you might begin your prayer saying:

"God, you are my Father. Because you sent your Son to pay the price for my sins, I am now able to approach you directly in prayer. I'm so thankful to be a part of your family.

"You're a good Father. You're so loving, faithful, true, just, merciful, patient, kind, slow to anger, affectionate, providing, and wise. I remember all the times you've been so good to me, when you _____, _____, and _____. Thank You so much for blessing me the way you have.

"Father, you sit on your throne in Heaven and you reign over all of your creation. I see through a glass darkly

but you see everything. Help me to learn to see things through your eyes, and help me to trust in you in those situations where my vision is limited, because I know yours is not.

"I praise you as Jehovah. You are I AM, my right-now God who will never change and will always be there for me. Father, you are the Lord my righteousness. By the shed blood of your Son, the Lord Jesus Christ, I can stand in your presence, not in any way due to my own righteousness, but by your righteousness which you've so graciously given to me. You are also Jehovah-M'Kaddesh, the Lord Who sanctifies me..."

Follow the outline in the Appendix so you can continue on through all nine of the redemptive names of God, focusing on the benefits each one provides and hallowing each of them through your praise. You shouldn't pray these prayer examples I've given you word-for-word, any more than you should pray the Lord's Prayer verbatim. Choose your own words and pray out of your own heart.

Hallowing His name in thanksgiving, praise and worship is a great way to open a prayer session. When we praise Him from our heart, His presence will be manifested. The Bible says that God inhabits the praises of His people (Psalms 22:3). Open your prayer like that and He will show up. Now, let me ask you a serious question:

Couldn't you do that for 10 minutes?

Why don't you take 10 minutes and try it right now? When you experience the reality of His presence, you're going to realize that someone has been lying to you, and you'll be amazed at how easy praying can be.

But we're just getting started! Now that you and your spiritual Partner are on the scene together, after you've both taken a few minutes to catch up and say hello, you're now ready to actually start getting some things done.

Chapter 5 Discussion Questions

1. How can "a personal relationship with God and a good understanding of His character" provide building blocks for an effective prayer life?

2. When might a Christian be tempted to pray "empty prayers"?

3. Often when we need to ask a favor from a friend, we'll start by flattering them: "You're so good at..." How is "hallowing" God's name different from buttering Him up?

4. How does God reveal His character through His names? What does the phrase "God revealing His character" mean to you?

5. *Why* does God choose to reveal Himself to us through His names?

6. How can an awareness of the redemptive names of God make our prayers more effective?

Chapter 6

Prayers of Power
Your Spiritual Support

Your kingdom come, your will be done, on earth as it is in heaven. - Matthew 6:10

When a person gets into trouble and needs some help, one of the first things we look at is what kinds of support systems does this person have? By support systems, we mean healthy relationships with people or organizations that are personally connected with the individual and can be counted on for support until the problems get resolved.

Support systems can include family and close friends, brothers and sisters within your local church congregation, and possibly other organizations in which you have established close friendships with other people. These might be sports teams, Scouting, social clubs, or even possibly at your job. However, as a Christian there's one support system you have which exceeds all others: the Kingdom of God.

What do we mean by the term "Kingdom of God?" Simply put, a kingdom is made up of all the areas where the King is in authority. The Bible teaches there are two spiritual kingdoms in this world (Colossians 1:13). These kingdoms are not in any way equal in power or authority.

The kingdom of darkness was completely spoiled by the Lord Jesus Christ:

He disarmed the rulers and authorities and put them to open shame, by triumphing over them in Him. - Colossians 2:15

The plan of redemption includes living with God throughout all eternity, but it's not limited to that. The full plan of redemption involves more than just your personal redemption. It also includes the transformation of the entire world, until the whole Earth is full of His glory (Psalms 72:19), culminating with the return of the Lord Jesus Christ.

Here's the exciting part: you have a role in helping to bring that to pass. As King, God the Father sits in the ultimate position of authority, but He has ordained that His people should operate in various areas of delegated authority under His rule. In this section of Jesus' teaching on how to pray, you'll be conducting Kingdom business within the areas of authority which God has entrusted to you.

Thy Kingdom Come

After He was anointed with the power of the Holy Spirit at His baptism and then tempted in the wilderness by the devil, Jesus immediately began to preach about the Kingdom of God.

From that time Jesus began to preach, saying, "Repent, for the kingdom of heaven is at hand." - Matthew 4:17

This message continued to be preached throughout His entire earthly ministry, and then was preached further still by His disciples, who were assigned the task of spreading His message through the church following His ascension (Acts 28:31). It continues to be preached today.

All authority was given to Jesus by the Father, and He delegated that authority to His followers who would go forth in His name (Matthew 28:18-20), a group that includes Christians today whether they realize it or not. As a believer in the Lord Jesus Christ, you have spiritual authority in His name over certain areas of your life.

First and foremost, you have the authority to ensure that the Kingdom of God is in force in your own life. Next, you have authority over your family if you're the head of your household. As a parent you have authority over your children until they come of age. If God has given you a place of authority in the workplace, you have a measure of spiritual authority there as well. Finally, whatever ministry God has called you to, with that calling He has also issued the spiritual authority necessary for you to carry it out.

Why is this important? Well, you can't enforce spiritual order in areas of your life where you don't have any authority to do so. For example, if a police officer signaled for you to pull your car over, you'd do it because he has the authority to instruct you to do that. However, if he ordered you to do something that he didn't have the authority to do, you wouldn't do it.

The same principle applies in prayer. People have been created with a free will, and most of the time you don't have the authority to force your choices on them. You might really think your neighbor should come to church on Sunday, but if you prayed and asked God to force them to attend, that wouldn't work. However, if you wanted your children in church you could make that happen, no matter how they felt about it, because you have spiritual authority over them.

Prayer can be divided into two basic categories: praying for yourself and praying for others. In order to be able to expand the Kingdom of God as we've been commanded, you're going to have to learn the right methods to pray for others.

Praying for the growth of the Kingdom in your own life is a simple matter, because you have full spiritual authority over yourself, but for others it's a different story. You can't just try to manipulate the will of others, through prayer, into doing what you want. In fact, that's technically a form of witchcraft. God doesn't operate that way, so that means you can't operate that way either.

Supplication and Intercession

So what is the correct way to pray for others? There are two kinds of prayer that can apply here: intercession and supplication. Which one you use depends on what type of person you're praying for. Just as Jesus put these prayers at the beginning of the prayer method He taught, the Apostle Paul also taught that these types of prayers should be prayed first, before praying about anything else.

FIRST OF ALL, then, I urge that supplications,

prayers, intercessions, and thanksgivings be made for all people, for kings and all who are in high positions, that we may lead a peaceful and quiet life, godly and dignified in every way.
  - I Timothy 2:1, 2

Let's define these two types of prayer. Supplication is prayer for those who are already in covenant with God, and currently living in good standing with Him. Intercession is prayer for those who are in rebellion, operating outside the boundaries of God's covenant. The rules for each type of prayer are different.

Intercession should be made for the following: unsaved people, believers who have backslidden in their faith, and national governments who are breaking God's laws. Scripture is clear that the judgment of God will fall upon all such people. The justice of God demands it, just as His justice demanded payment for your sins.

Jesus is the original intercessor between God and man (I Timothy 2:5). He willingly stood between us and the judgment we deserved, and bridged the gap between us and the Father.

Through intercessory prayer you become an extension of Jesus' ministry of intercession, placing yourself between those sinners and the judgment that surely awaits them if they don't change, praying that God would grant them mercy and a space of time so they might repent.

Supplication is similar to intercession in that you are

still praying for others, but in this case these are people who are not headed toward judgment because they've already repented of their sins. There are specific ways you can pray and certain scriptures you can stand on for those who are safely under the umbrella of protection of God's covenant which don't apply to those who are not.

Supplication prayers can be made for anyone who is currently in covenant with the Lord, including ministers, fellow Christians, and direct family members, as well as national leaders. The Bible teaches that God has a unique relationship with men and women who rule nations, whether they are Christians or not, by virtue of the office they hold (Romans 13:1).

Praying the prayer of supplication for others is similar to praying the prayer of petition (covered in chapter 7) for yourself, because in both kinds of prayer you're standing on promises found in the Word of God. Some Bible examples of the prayer of supplication can be found in Ephesians 1:15-21, 3:14-21, and Colossians 1:9-12.

Thy Will Be Done

The followers of Jesus routinely misunderstood His teaching about the coming Kingdom of God, expecting an earthly kingdom that would begin with the overthrow of Roman rule over Israel, instead of a spiritual kingdom that would begin within the hearts of men. When Jesus realized this, He taught them the *Parable of the Talents*.

As they heard these things, he proceeded to tell a parable, because he was near to Jerusalem, and

because they supposed that the kingdom of God was to appear immediately. – Luke 19:11

In this parable, Jesus (represented by the nobleman) is going away for a long time. He assigns tasks to His servants, giving each of them the necessary resources to fulfill His instructions. Then He told them to get to work and He departed.

And he called his ten servants, and delivered them ten pounds, and said unto them, Occupy till I come. – Luke 19:13 (KJV)

This is still our assigned task today. As you seek ways to expand the Kingdom of God within your own sphere of influence, you should be continuously, successfully, and progressively invading the kingdom of darkness and occupying new territory for Him. This is the wide-angle lens view of the will of God for your life.

When you pray for the Kingdom of God to be expanded in your life, first start with your nation, including your city, state and national political leaders. Pray according to I Timothy 1:1-2 that conditions in the world would be peaceful in order to better facilitate the spreading of the Gospel. Finally, pray for the peace of Jerusalem (Psalms 122:6).

Next start praying that God's kingdom would come and His will would be done in your own life, and work your way outward from there. Exercise the authority God has given you by praying that the Kingdom would come into your life, into the life of your spouse, the lives of your children, as well as other family members.

Continue by praying for your church. Pray for your Pastor and the leadership of your local congregation. Pray for the people in the church, that they would be faithful and walk in love and unity. Finally pray for the harvest of souls that's out there just waiting to be brought in.

Most of this section of our prayer pattern deals with praying for others, and when you're praying for yourself in this phase, you're basically praying a prayer of submission to God's will for your life. It's the same kind of prayer that Jesus prayed at Gethsemane:

"Father, if you are willing, remove this cup from me. Nevertheless, not my will, but yours, be done." - Luke 22:42

It's extremely important to be submitted to God's will for your life. It's worth remembering that when the Nobleman finally returned at the end of the Parable of the Talents, all the servants had to give an account of what they'd done with the authority He'd given them to use. Likewise, we will give an account of what we've done with the resources He's given us.

On Earth As In Heaven

Notice that as you're praying to God about all these things, you're saying to Him, "Your will be done." Not your own will, not the will of man, and certainly not the devil's will, but rather that the will of God alone would be done. Now here's a good question: how can you know what the will of God is?

Praying outside the will of God won't work. The Apostle John says that any prayers that are not in agreement with His will won't even get a hearing in the court of Heaven, but if we do get a hearing then we can be confident that we'll also receive an answer.

And this is the confidence that we have toward him, that if we ask anything according to his will he hears us. And if we know that he hears us in whatever we ask, we know that we have the requests that we have asked of him.
- I John 5:14, 15

Obviously, it's incredibly important that we pray according to His will, but how can we know what God's will actually is? The question of the will of God is something Christians have struggled with and theologians have debated for centuries. How can you possibly be expected to figure it out?

Actually, it's much simpler than you might think. The written Word of God contains His will, and while it may take some time for you to discern God's will in the very specific areas of your life, the Bible covers the will of God over a large range of general areas.

Another really useful guideline to discovering the will of God for you and those within your spiritual authority can be found right in the midst Jesus' prayer teaching, yet it is very often overlooked:

Your kingdom come, your will be done, on earth as it is in heaven. - Matthew 6:10

If you're ever unsure about the will of God in a particular area of life, take a moment to consider how it works in Heaven for that same area. After all, here on earth there are sinful people who choose to rebel against Him, so His will is not always done here. If it was, why would Jesus instruct us to pray for it? But in Heaven the will of God is carried out without question and without delay.

So when you wonder how you should go about praying, "Thy kingdom come, thy will be done" for a certain person or problem, think about how it is in Heaven. For example, if you're praying for a friend who's sick, what is the will of God on the subject? Well, is there any sickness in Heaven? No? Then you should pray "on Earth as it is in Heaven," that there would be no sickness in your friend's body.

What if you're praying for someone who's confused? Is there any confusion in Heaven? How about a person who's struggling with unexpected financial challenges? Is there any lack in Heaven? What about that relative who's fighting depression and anxiety? You get the idea. Based on what the Bible has revealed about Heaven alone, you can start to get a much clearer picture of God's will very quickly.

Summary

As believers we are citizens of the country we live in here on Earth, but we are also citizens of the Kingdom of God. We have dual-citizenship, and just as you have rights by virtue of being a citizen of your country, so you also have rights and authority which you can exercise as a subject of the Kingdom.

If it's true that it's not what you know, but rather who you know, then you should rejoice because it so happens that you know Someone in very high places. You're connected. When the topic of Heaven comes up, one of your first thoughts should be, "I've got people there."

Because of that, you can pray for the expansion of the Kingdom of God here on Earth, touching every realm where you have been given spiritual authority. For example, you might pray:

"God, I take authority over every aspect of my life today in the name of Jesus. Kingdom of God, come into my life today. Will of God, be done in my life today. I pray your kingdom would reign over my heart today, over my thoughts and over my words.

"May the kingdom have rule over my body, and the will of God be done concerning my healing. Let your kingdom come into my finances today, and the will of God be done there.

"God, I want my marriage to be under kingdom rule, and may your will be done in my calling as a husband. Kingdom of God, come into my wife's life today, and reveal to her your divine will.

"Let me also do your will as a father, and may your kingdom have influence over the lives of my children. Protect them as they go forth, and work your will and good

pleasure in them today.

"I pray for my unsaved neighbor, that you would reveal your Word to him and draw him to yourself by your Holy Spirit. I pray that you would send laborers across his path, people who he will listen and give place to. I bind the devil who would blind his eyes to the light of the glorious Gospel, so that he will not be deceived about the choice that lies before him."

Continue onward, touching on all the areas in your life where you have the authority to pray. Once again, follow the outline in Appendix A on page 173 for this second section of the prayer pattern Jesus taught.

Obviously, if you're a wife, then you will switch the words "husband" and "wife." If you're not married, your prayer will also need to be worded differently. Use my examples above to give you an idea of what you might say, but when you pray come up with your own words and speak them out of your own heart.

As with the first section of our prayer pattern, it should now be clear to you that you'll have no problem filling up ten minutes of time praying along these lines. In fact, you'd better keep an eye on the clock if you have only an hour of time available to pray, because you can very easily find yourself praying in this section alone for 20-30 minutes or longer.

Just like you did at the end of chapter 5, take ten minutes right now and try praying through this section.

There's a good Bible lesson which uses an acrostic of the word J-O-Y to describe how we as believers should set our priorities in order to find true joy in our lives: put (J)esus first, (O)thers second, and (Y)ourself last.

So far you've opened up your prayer with praise to the Father in Heaven, recognizing His position and hallowing His name. Next you've submitted yourself to God's will and prayed for everybody else in the world, that His kingdom would come and His will would be done on Earth as it is in Heaven.

After focusing on God and others, now you're ready for a good hard look at your own wants and needs. It's time to take care of some business.

Chapter 6 Discussion Questions

1. Why do Christians sometimes struggle to recognize the kingdom of God as a capable support system?

2. God has a global plan for the whole world and He also has plans for our everyday walk. How do we maintain our daily walk so it fits in with His big plan? How do our little steps help bring His larger plan to fruition?

3. When a police officer pulls you over, you have the right to verify his authority by calling 911 or checking his badge to confirm his ID. What is the badge of authority for you as a believer? How do we check that we are still within the bounds of our authority in the circumstances in which we want to pray to bring about changes?

4. As it relates to the believer's authority, why is it necessary to understand God's redemptive plan?

5. Why is it important to recognize the difference between supplication and intercession? How are these two kinds of prayer similar? In what ways are they different?

6. What are some of the things God always wants? How does knowing His general will help us when we need to determine His specific will in a particular area?

Chapter 7

Prayers of Petition
Taking Care of Business

"Give us this day our daily bread," - Matthew 6:11

The first two sections of the prayer pattern Jesus taught focused on God the Father:

After this manner therefore pray ye: Our Father which art in heaven, Hallowed be thy name. Thy kingdom come, Thy will be done in earth, as it is in heaven. - Matthew 6:9, 10 (KJV)

With this third section of the blueprint, which can be found in Matthew 6:11 and Luke 11:3, the spotlight moves off of God and onto the person who's doing the praying. Praying for yourself can be tricky sometimes.

On the one hand, you want to make sure you're successful getting what you need to get done, taking full advantage of the inheritance the Lord Jesus Christ won for you on the cross. After all, if He paid such a price to deliver these benefits of the New Covenant to you, would it not be a slap in His face to adopt a posture of false humility and tell Him, "No, that's okay. Thanks anyway, Jesus."

On the other hand, you don't want to be selfish either. You know that in J-O-Y, yourself comes last. If you pray from a motive of greed and covetousness, you know it's not going to work because God will see right through it. The real worry isn't that God will notice your selfishness however, but rather you failing to be aware of it. The Bible is full of verses cautioning us to not let our hearts deceive us.

Take care lest your heart be deceived, and you turn aside and serve other gods and worship them; - Deuteronomy 11:16

When we think of serving other gods, we often imagine primitive people kneeling before a wooden idol or something like that. However, the truth is our society is full of idols today, and one of them is covetousness.

Put to death therefore what is earthly in you: sexual immorality, impurity, passion, evil desire, and covetousness, which is idolatry. - Colossians 3:5

As we will see in this chapter, God doesn't mind your having things. He just doesn't want things to have you! The question then becomes how can we walk this line between coming to God to get all of our wants and needs met, without crossing over that line into selfishness? The answer is to approach praying for your needs from a perspective of enlightened self-interest.

To use a natural example, have you ever flown on an airplane and listened to the flight attendants go through their routine about the oxygen masks? If the oxygen masks drop and you have children, what they tell you to do is put your mask on first before you try to put oxygen masks on any of your children.

This sounds very selfish at first, until they explain that if you try to put the masks on the children before putting yours on, you could pass out from lack of oxygen and then nobody will get their masks on. In that situation you have to look out for your own enlightened self-interest first so that you'll then be in a position to look out for the interests of those around you.

The enemy will do everything he can to keep you sick, poor and depressed. If you're tired and sick all the time, then you won't have any energy to do the work of the Lord. If you don't have enough money to pay your bills, you won't have any to spare for the ministries God has connected to you. If you're depressed, you won't have the motivation to serve Him.

You have to make sure you're getting what you require from God regarding your healing, provision, peace and whatever else you may need. Otherwise you won't be in any state to be a help or be a blessing to those who are around you. You have to put your own spiritual oxygen mask on first.

Believe God Wants To Bless You

When it comes to bringing your petitions to the Father, one of the biggest mental barriers you have to get past is the idea that poverty and sickness are somehow humble or godly. This is an evil religious tradition that has no basis in the Scriptures at all, yet it's deeply ingrained in our thinking and in many of our churches.

God's will is that we experience both healing and financial success, with the understanding that we're supposed to be continuing to grow spiritually at the same time:

Beloved, I pray that you may prosper in all things and be in health, just as your soul prospers.
- III John 2 (NKJ)

True humility is to submit your mind to God's Word, and to change your thinking when your ideas and God's Word disagree (Romans 12:2). The Bible doesn't say money is the root of all evil. It says the love of money is the root of all evil (I Timothy 6:10). You can commit that sin and not have one thin dime in your pocket.

As far as healing goes, we read in the Word how Jesus went everywhere healing the sick (Acts 10:38). Did He ever once lay His hands on someone to put sickness upon them? We can look at what Jesus did and see the will of the Father, because Jesus said, "Whoever has seen me has seen the Father" (John 14:9).

For that matter, we can look back to what we learned in the last chapter concerning the will of God, where we prayed, *"Thy will be done in earth, as it is in heaven"* (Matthew 6:9). Is there any sickness in Heaven? Is anyone in Heaven worried about being able to pay their light bill this month? If Heaven is the place where the will of God is carried out perfectly, and if there's no sickness or lack there, that tells you all you need to know about the will of God, doesn't it?

If God told you that He wanted you healthy and strong so you'd have the energy to do the things He's called you to do, financially successful so you'd have the resources to do what He's called you to do, and have the peace of mind to not worry about what He's called you to do, would you be able to humble yourself to accept His will for you without feeling guilty about it?

The fact is He's already told you all of that in His Word. The Word of God is the will of God. He wants to bless you, and if you're going to be able to approach Him and pray, "Give us this day our daily bread," then you must believe that.

Petition Guidelines

The prayer of petition (sometimes referred to as the prayer of faith) is a prayer you'll be praying often, because new needs and challenges will continue to arise every day. Remember reading in chapter 2 about how there are different rules for different kinds of prayers, just like there are different rules for different sports? Certain guidelines must be followed when delivering petitions to the Father in prayer.

Decide What You Want

The first step in praying a petition prayer is deciding exactly what you want. What do you want? Don't say "whatever" if specific is what you need. Be specific. Take note of the order of the words in Mark 11:24:

Therefore I say unto you, What things soever ye desire, when ye pray, believe that ye receive them, and ye shall have them. - Mark 11:24 (KJV)

Jesus said that whatever it is that you desire from God, that desire actually happens first. *"What things soever you desire",* comes before *"when ye pray."* Don't go bringing a petition into the Father's presence without first knowing exactly what you want, and don't short change yourself.

If it's going to take $567.23 to pay for that car repair, don't pray, "God, just give me what You think I should have." If you're about to pray for a car and you have a certain make and model in mind, but you want a red one, then pray for that make and model in red.

What do you desire? Notice I didn't say "need." Some people believe God will meet your needs, but you're on your own when it comes to your desires. However, God makes no distinction between your needs and your wants. If you come to Him with a request, He doesn't check first to see if it's a need or a desire.

In fact, by definition, a need is already a desire. If I need oxygen to breathe, then don't I also automatically desire oxygen? If I have to have a certain amount of money to pay my bills each month, don't I also desire that?

God doesn't distinguish between needs and desires. That's a religious tradition rooted in a false concept of humility that Satan slipped into church doctrine during the Middle Ages.

"But what if I pray for something selfishly?" If you do, then the prayer won't work because your heart wouldn't be right. This isn't a formula. It's not a mathematical equation. It's a heart matter, and you know when your heart is right and when it isn't.

As we continue, we'll see that there are some qualifiers Jesus places on the prayer of petition, but nowhere does He ever say anything like, "Now, these have to be real needs, and I mean desperate needs. Don't come to Me praying for things you don't need!"

You won't find that anywhere in the Bible, yet sadly millions of Christians all over the world believe it today. Instead, Jesus says:

Fear not, little flock, for it is your Father's good pleasure to give you the kingdom. - Luke 12:32

Jesus said, *"What things soever you desire"*. What do you desire? Apparently He trusts you, so why don't you trust yourself? Step one is to decide exactly what you want.

According to the Word

However, God will always check to see whether your request is in line with His Word. The Word of God is the will of God. If you're praying against the Word, then you're praying against His will, and your prayer won't get a hearing in Heaven's throne room.

And this is the confidence that we have toward him, that if we ask anything according to his will he hears us. And if we know that he hears us in whatever we ask, we know that we have the requests that we have asked of him. - I John 5:14, 15

If we pray according to His will, then He hears us, and if we know He hears us then we know our request will be granted. What happens if we don't pray according to the Word?

If one turns away his ear from hearing the law (the Word), **even his prayer is an abomination.** - **Proverbs 28:9**

What if you petitioned God for a spouse who was already married to someone else? Would that prayer get answered? Of course it wouldn't be granted, because clearly it's not God's will to break up a good marriage just to get you a partner.

In order to make sure you're praying according to His will, you're going to have to find scriptures where God has already promised what you're requesting. For example, you might petition God for healing based on I Peter 2:24, or for money to pay a bill based on Philippians 4:19.

If you abide in me, AND MY WORDS ABIDE IN YOU, ask whatever you wish, and it will be done for you. - **John 15:7**

The second step in praying the prayer of petition is finding Bible verses that cover your request.

Ask

Once you've decided exactly what you want, the third step is to ask. A surprisingly large number of Christians don't believe you need to ask because God already knows what you need before you even pray.

God certainly does know what you need, probably better than you do. He is God, after all. So what? He still commands us to ask:

ASK, and it will be given to you; seek, and you will find; knock, and it will be opened to you. For everyone who asks receives, and the one who seeks finds, and to the one who knocks it will be opened. - Matthew 7:7, 8

And all things, whatsoever ye shall ASK in prayer, believing, ye shall receive. - Matthew 21:22 (KJV)

You did not choose me, but I chose you and appointed you that you should go and bear fruit and that your fruit should abide, so that whatever you ASK the Father in my name, he may give it to you. - John 15:16

In that day you will ask nothing of me. Truly, truly, I say to you, whatever you ASK of the Father in my name, he will give it to you. Until now you have asked nothing in my name. ASK, and you will receive, that your joy may be full.
- John 16:23, 24

If any of you lacks wisdom, let him ASK God, who gives generously to all without reproach, and it will be given him. - James 1:5

You desire and do not have, so you murder. You covet and cannot obtain, so you fight and quarrel. You do not have, because you do not ASK. - James 4:2

Not only do you have to ask, but you need to ask with the proper motives. Whether it's a need or a desire, you can't ask with a wrong heart.

You ask and do not receive, because you ask wrongly, to spend it on your passions. - James 4:3

Step #3 for petition prayers is you must ask.

Believe You Receive

The next step is to believe you receive. When you pray, believe that you have the thing that you prayed for. When do you believe you receive it? When it shows up at your door?

Therefore I say unto you, What things soever ye desire, WHEN YOU PRAY, believe that ye receive them, and ye shall have them. - Mark 11:24 (KJV)

No, according to Jesus you are to believe you receive when you pray. If you waited until the answer to your prayer was sitting in front of you, you wouldn't need to believe you receive because you'd be looking at it. Step #4 is to believe you receive when you pray.

Thank God For The Answer

The final step in the prayer of petition is to thank God for the answer to your prayer. You see, after you pray and believe you receive, some time may pass before the answer arrives. Spiritually, you received the answer when you prayed. Yet in the natural realm it may not have manifested yet. I call that the time between the "amen" and the "there it is." You're going to have to stay in faith while you're waiting for the answer to arrive.

Now, there are a couple of things you have to remember while you're standing in faith. The first thing is you don't want to ask God for the same thing over and over again. If you asked for what you wanted and you truly believed you received it when you prayed, then why would you ask for it a second, third and fourth time? Don't you believe what Jesus said? He said when you pray and believe you receive, then you shall have the answer.

But let him ask in faith, with no doubting, for he who doubts is like a wave of the sea driven and tossed by the wind. For let not that man suppose that he will receive anything from the Lord; he is a double-minded man, unstable in all his ways. - James 1:6-8

Asking over and over for the same thing is an indication of double-mindedness, and the Bible states that a person like that shouldn't think he's going to receive anything from the Lord. So what should you do if you've prayed, and some time has passed, and the answer to your prayer still hasn't appeared?

Instead of asking again for something you've already believed you've received, just thank God for it by faith. Thank Him because you know He heard your prayer, because you know He's faithful to His Word, and because you know the answer is on its way.

The second thing to remember is you can resist doubt with thanksgiving. During this time between the "amen" and the "there it is," the enemy is going to do everything he can to shake your faith. If he can get you to waiver, then he can undo your prayer and prevent you from receiving. You can stay in faith by thanking God for the answer, even before you see it with your eyes.

For we walk by faith, not by sight.
– II Corinthians 5:7

Why does it matter whether you follow the rules for the prayer of petition as they are outlined in the Word of God? Is God going to deny your request if you deviate from those guidelines? Is He just looking for some reason to avoid answering your prayer? That's not the case at all.

The problem is there's a spiritual outlaw, named Satan, who wants to hinder your spiritual progress by blocking your prayers if he can. But when you carry out your petition in accordance with the Word of God, your obedience boxes the enemy in and prevents him from being able to interfere.

Start A Prayer Journal

In the political world, before online petitions became popular, petitions were typically written down on paper. I'm sure you've heard about petitions that gather signatures for a political cause Sometimes a petition will be started to prevent a television show from being cancelled. In each of those cases, the petition is something that's written out.

Remember the illustration of your daily phone call with the President in chapter 1? If you really were doing a daily call like that with him, would you take a few moments before the call to jot down some notes, or would you just wing it? I'm sure you'd at least make a list of the things you wanted to ask him for, if for no other reason, so you wouldn't accidentally forget something.

When you go into a meeting at work with your boss, do you just talk off the top of your head, or do you make some notes before the meeting so you'll be prepared when it starts? If something important is said during the meeting, would you jot it down or just trust your memory to retain it?

Of course you know the answer is to take good notes. If you'd do that for a meeting with people, why wouldn't you do it for your all-knowing and all-wise God? There's a principle I've learned to live by: "If it doesn't get written down, it never happened."

First, making notes helps you to be specific. Taking a few minutes to write down your requests will help you to get the wording just the way you want it. You can also write down the scriptures you're standing on.

Second, making notes in your journal will help you remember what you prayed for. While you're waiting for the thing you've believed you received to manifest, you'll want to stay in faith, and resist doubt and unbelief, by thanking God for granting you the thing that you've asked Him for. It's easy to thank God for those things when you have them all written there in your prayer journal.

The third and greatest benefit of a journal is over time it will transform into a record of your prayer victories. As each thing you've petitioned for arrives, mark off that item and put down the date when it came to pass. Reviewing these answered prayers will strengthen your faith while you wait for other things you've prayed for.

This will also help to increase your faith to believe God for even greater things. One of the reasons David had the faith to face Goliath was because of his previous victories in battle (I Samuel 17:34-36). Once you have a few prayer victories under your belt, like David, you'll be ready to step out and take on even greater challenges. Keeping a simple prayer journal is a very practical step that will help you track your spiritual victories.

Summary

Jesus taught us to pray, *"Give us this day our daily our daily bread."* The very words of that sentence reveal how He desires for us to talk to the Father about our wants and needs on a daily basis.

This is one of the easiest sections of the prayer blueprint to pray through for the full ten minutes. If you have any faith at all, it isn't going to take you much time to come up with a long list of things you can petition God for. This is where the prayer journal will be especially helpful to you:

"Lord, I thank you that Your Word says in I Peter 2:24 that by Jesus' stripes I was healed. Sickness has been trying to jump on me, but right now I believe I receive my healing, and I thank you for it."

Continue like this for whatever else you want to ask of God. For those things that you've already asked Him for, thank Him that they have been done and are on the way even now:

"I also want to thank You again for sending me that money I need to pay off this loan and get out of debt, according to Philippians 4;19 and Romans 13:8. I know it's on the way because You are faithful to Your promises, and You've never let me down."

When you're first getting started, your list of petitions might not be very long. If your list is too short, spend some time during this 10-minute section praying about what other things God would have you add to your list. Think about what you're going to need to carry out the things He's called you to do, find scripture verses that cover them, and bring your petitions to Him.

Take 10 minutes now to pray your own version of *"Give us this day our daily bread."* Talk to Him about what you want and why you want it. Ask for it based on scripture passages you know that cover those desires. This is also a great way to improve your personal Bible study time, as you'll be motivated to seek a greater knowledge of the Word so you can pray more effectively.

Now that you've taken some time to think this through, and you have a very clear picture of what you need to have coming down to you from Heaven's pipeline, the next section of the prayer outline will help you make sure that conduit from Heaven to you stays clear.

Chapter 7 Discussion Questions

1. Good parents will meet the wants and needs of their child if they can, even if it means they must do without to make it happen. Does God need to do without something in order to meet the wants and needs of His children? What does that mean for His willingness to give good things to His children?

2. How can the oxygen mask on the airplane illustration help us distinguish between enlightened self-interest and selfishness?

3. Why is it vital to *know exactly* what you desire from God?

4. What would you do if you ordered a package and never received it? Would you forget about it? Would you assume it must not be the will of UPS or FedEx for you to have it? How does keeping a prayer journal help you keep track of "packages" you're still waiting to receive?

5. When Jesus spoke the words, "Give us this day our daily bread," technology did not exist to store food like we do today. Before preservatives were discovered, bread had to be made daily or it would spoil. When looking at Jesus' words in this context, what are the implications for our daily prayer experience?

6. How could an inability to address our needs and desires through prayer have an impact on others?

Chapter 8

Prayers of Submission
Performing Spiritual Maintenance

"And forgive us our debts, as we also have forgiven our debtors." - Matthew 6:12

Having started with our focus on the Lord, His name, His Kingdom, and His will, we have now moved into the portion of the prayer outline that focuses on us. In the last chapter we looked at the prayer of petition, where we brought our personal needs and desires before Him in prayer. Now we're going to look at another crucial aspect of our spiritual lives: repentance and forgiveness.

It's interesting to me how Jesus organized the prayer pattern that He taught. If there was an issue in your life where God's forgiveness was required, most people would agree that you should take care of that before you start trying to talk to God about any personal desires you have. However, Jesus didn't do it that way.

He has you start with God and His Kingdom, and then proceed from there to pray for yourself as an individual. However, when you get to this section of the prayer where you're praying about yourself, Jesus wants you to address the physical needs of your day first, before trying to deal with any sin or unforgiveness. Doesn't that seem backwards to you?

I would think that if there was any sin in my life, I ought to get that out of the way first, and then once I was clear from that I could go on to pray about these other things. That's how I thought about it for a long time. Most people would agree with this approach, but not Jesus.

I submit to you this proposal: if you can begin to understand the reasons why Jesus put things in this particular order in His prayer pattern, you will be much closer to understanding God's perspective on life as a whole and the way He thinks about you and the world.

Now it should go without saying that Christians shouldn't sin, but let me take a moment to remind you anyway. Sin looks like a lot of fun at first. There is pleasure to be found in sin for a season (Hebrews 11:25). If there wasn't, then it wouldn't be a temptation, would it? Yet in the end, sin will kill you.

For the wages of sin is death, but the free gift of God is eternal life in Christ Jesus our Lord.
   - Romans 6:23

Sin is what separated us from the Father to begin with, but thank God for the free gift of eternal life in Christ Jesus. We've been set free from the power that sin had over us, and yet there will be times when we will still miss God and commit sins during our Christian walk.

What is God's point of view? The Bible says that

it's the goodness of God that leads men to repentance. It's not getting yelled at, or judged, or beat over the head that makes people repent. It's His goodness.

Or do you despise the riches of His goodness, forbearance, and longsuffering, not knowing that the goodness of God leads you to repentance? - Romans 2:4 (NKJ)

So here you are, three sections of your prayer blueprint prayed through, halfway done with your prayer hour. You spent the first portion telling Your Father how wonderful He is and hallowing His name. You spent the next part declaring His sovereignty over every area of your life.

Then you spent the third section talking to Him about your wants and desires, and thanking Him both for the answers that are on the way and the answers that have manifested. The whole prayer outline up to this point has been a celebration of the goodness of God, building up to a crescendo of appreciation and thankfulness in your heart.

Having achieved that state of mind, in that spiritual environment, now He tells you to ask for forgiveness if you need it. How smart is our God! How wise are His ways. After immersing yourself in His goodness for three full sections of your prayer blueprint, now you're in a position to come to a place of repentance if necessary, but how you got here is important.

You didn't start your prayer wallowing in your mistakes and regrets, consumed by self-pity and focused on yourself. Instead, you started out focusing on Him and His goodness, so the path that you've followed to this place of repentance is the way He chose to bring you. Praise God!

Condemnation

Still, sin is a problem. It short-circuits our connection with the Father. We've already looked at Hebrews 4:16, which tells us to come boldly to the throne of grace:

> **Let us then with confidence draw near to the throne of grace, that we may receive mercy and find grace to help in time of need.**
> **- Hebrews 4:16**

If there is sin in your life, you will feel self-conscious about it when you enter into the presence of God. Exposed to His holiness and purity, your sin will stand out in stark contrast, and because of this, it will be difficult for you to draw near to Him with bold confidence.

When there is unconfessed sin in your life it will hinder you from receiving from God. How does this happen? Does God get mad at us and shut us out until we make it right? Maybe the devil gains the power to block our prayers when we sin? Actually, neither of these is the reason.

To find out who's responsible for sin hindering your prayers, go take a look in the mirror. The person you see there is the one who is the cause. The reason sin hinders your prayer life is this: when you sin, it is your own heart that condemns you.

> **Beloved, if our heart does not condemn us, we have confidence before God; and whatever we ask we receive from him, because we keep his commandments and do what pleases him.**
> **- I John 3:21, 22**

Another thing that can hinder you, besides sin, is what the Bible calls "weights." Weights are things in your life that aren't sins, but they still weigh you down spiritually. When you have too much physical weight, it saps your strength and prevents you from being able to move quickly. Spiritual weights do the same thing in your spirit. The Bible says it's very easy for these weights to get attached to our lives:

> **Therefore, since we are surrounded by so great a cloud of witnesses, let us also lay aside every weight, and sin which clings so closely, and let us run with endurance the race that is set before us, - Hebrews 12:1**

Weights are not "little" sins. Instead, we should think of them as things in our lifestyle that could hinder our Christian walk. It could be a job, other obligations, or even a hobby. When we pray, we need to ask God to reveal to us any weights that are hindering us and require our attention.

God isn't the one beating you up because of your sin. Your own conscience condemns you, and when it does, you are left with no confidence to stand before God. On the other hand, if your heart doesn't condemn you, then you will have that confidence when you go before Him, and the Bible promises that whatever you ask from Him you will receive. So let's start working on getting that confidence back.

Asking Forgiveness

As Christians, we don't sin habitually like we did when we were unsaved. Our spirits have been reborn (John 3:3) and recreated (II Corinthians 5:17), and though we may still commit sin occasionally, as we continue to grow in grace and sanctification, sinning becomes the exception rather than the rule in our lives.

No one born of God makes a practice of sinning, for God's seed abides in him, and he cannot keep on sinning because he has been born of God.
- I John 3:9

However, we still have a mind that needs to be renewed and an unredeemed body that will be full of fleshly desires until we leave this world or until Jesus returns. We don't want sin to happen, but there will be times when we miss it in our Christian walk. The moment we realize that we have sinned, we must immediately repent.

If we confess our sins, he is faithful and just to forgive us our sins and to cleanse us from all unrighteousness. - I John 1:9

When you mess up, don't run from God. Run to Him. Throw yourself on His mercy and receive your forgiveness by faith, not because of anything you did to deserve it, but because of what Jesus did in your place. Be quick to repent. If you are, you typically won't enter the hour of prayer with your sins on your mind.

Yet, as you're praying through the prayer outline, your heightened awareness of the goodness of God may lead you to recognize for the first time certain areas of your life in which repentance is required, areas that you never noticed before. This will happen to you. When it does, ask for forgiveness accordingly.

God doesn't expect you to be perfect. You don't have to learn the entire Bible and be on top of everything all at once. You will grow into spiritual maturity. When you begin, you're responsible for only the things that you know.

But if we walk in the light, as he is in the light, we have fellowship with one another, and the blood of Jesus his Son cleanses us from all sin.
- I John 1:7

As you grow and get more light on the Word of God, you'll progressively become aware of new areas in your life that you need to address, but it's a process. Thank God that He doesn't show us everything we need to fix in our lives all at once! We surely wouldn't be able to handle it.

Instead, He brings us along a little bit at a time, gradually opening new areas of our lives and shining the light of His Word there. That's why it is so vitally important to keep the channel of communication between you and God open.

When communications are down due to sin, you can't hear from God to receive the direction you need for your spiritual growth to continue. When God reveals to you a new area of your life where you need to make some changes, repent immediately.

The moment you become aware of sin in your life or being out of step with God's will, take steps to set it aright. The strength of your connection to Him will determine how effectively you'll be able to walk in the authority He's given you, how easily you will receive answers to prayer, and how clearly you will get direction from Him for your life.

Satan knows this all too well, so his goal is to tempt you to commit sin so he can disrupt that vertical link, from you up to the Father, with guilt and condemnation. If he is unable to disrupt the vertical flow of spiritual life between you and the Father, then he has a backup plan: to disrupt the horizontal flow of life between you and the people around you.

Granting Forgiveness

We live in a fallen world full of devils, demons, and crazy people. Sometimes people, even Christians at times, will yield to temptation and allow themselves to be used by those evil spirits, thereby causing harm to others. Sometimes you will be the person who yields to the evil spirits. If you do, repent as soon as you realize what you're doing.

However, if demons are using someone to act out against you, you must forgive that person. Jesus said we have to forgive. He commanded us to pray:

"And forgive us our debts, as we also have forgiven our debtors." - Matthew 6:12

Note the words "as we also." What happens if we don't "also" forgive others? The clear implication is we won't be able to obtain our own forgiveness. In the other passage where He taught this prayer pattern, Jesus said to pray:

"And forgive us our sins, for we ourselves forgive everyone who is indebted to us." - Luke 11:4

The wording here suggests that the very reason we're able to ask for forgiveness is because we've already forgiven those people who have mistreated us. Following right behind the great prayer promise of Mark 11:24, we read these verses:

"And whenever you stand praying, if you have anything against anyone, forgive him, that your Father in heaven may also forgive you your trespasses. But if you do not forgive, neither will your Father in heaven forgive your trespasses." - Mark 11:25, 26

What we learn from these verses is that our ability to receive forgiveness is dependent on our obedience to Jesus' command to forgive others. If you want to keep the channel between you and the Father open, then you must forgive. Unforgiveness will prevent you from receiving answers to your prayers.

Yet, if we're honest, granting forgiveness to those

who have hurt us can be very difficult to do. I've spent time counselling with many different believers who were struggling with unforgiveness.

I showed them Bible verses like the ones above, and I tried to get them to understand the necessity of forgiveness, but they wouldn't do it. Even after seeing it in black and white in the Word of God, they ignored the truth and refused to obey.

What never occurred to them, what they didn't even realize, was that they weren't hurting the individuals from whom they were withholding their forgiveness. They were hurting only themselves.

Holding on to unforgiveness is like telling the person who hurt you, "I'll show you!" and then drinking poison. You aren't harming the one you're angry at, but you're killing yourself spiritually because you're allowing the unforgiveness to separate you from the Father.

Forgiveness Is A Command

So, how do you overcome unforgiveness when it's in your heart? I remember the first time I learned this lesson. I was saved at the age of 10 and filled with the Spirit when I was 16. When I was 15 I had a friend in high school who caused some major problems in my life. Without going into all the details, suffice it to say he lied to me and the result when it all finally came out left me feeling hurt, embarrassed, and extremely angry.

Every time the thought of this person or the situation

would cross my mind, I would become furious inside. I was so angry at him that I fantasized about killing him. I would literally daydream about sneaking into his bedroom while he was asleep at night and slitting his throat. I pictured how I would do it, by climbing the tree beside his house, and climbing up their roof so I could slip into his bedroom window.

I remember thinking to myself that he had a dog that liked to bark, so I'd have to do something about the dog. I planned out how I could take a poisoned piece of meat with me to take care of the dog when I went over there to kill this person. Then I started working out how I might go about obtaining the poison.

About that time I'd catch myself, realize what I was doing, and say, "You're supposed to be a Christian, you can't let yourself be thinking things like that!" Granted, I was only 15 years old, but, still I knew better, and I was still responsible to answer to God for allowing those thoughts to run through my head.

I share the details of this story simply to get across to you how unbelievably angry I was at that time. Forgiveness was the farthest thing from my mind. Yet, even as a young Baptist boy, I sensed the Holy Spirit speaking to me, "You're going to have to forgive him." I thought, "There's no way." But then I'd also think about scriptures like Mark 11:25 and 26, and I knew if I didn't forgive him it would block me from receiving my own forgiveness.

What was I going to do? I pled my case with the Lord. I told Him that He knew what this person had done, and because He was God, He knew my heart.

He knew how I felt inside. I told the Lord, "If I say I forgive him when we both know I'm really feeling the way I feel, it would be a lie, and I won't lie to You." Then the Lord showed me the secret to being able to forgive, even in that extreme circumstance.

By His Spirit, He spoke to my heart and said, "I gave you a command: to forgive. I never said anything about what you should or shouldn't feel. I just told you what I wanted you to do. The only question here is, will you obey Me?" That's when I saw it: that forgiveness was, at its root, a choice whether or not to be obedient, and it had nothing to do with my feelings.

So I prayed, "Alright, Lord. You know how I feel. If I could kill him and not suffer any consequences, I'd do it." There's no point in sugar coating things with God. He already knows the thoughts and intents of your heart, so while you always want to be reverent and respectful, at the same time you might as well just be brutally honest with Him. You'll be able to move along faster spiritually when you're honest with yourself and honest with Him.

I continued, "But You commanded me to forgive him, and when I asked You into my heart I didn't just pray for You to be my Savior. I asked You to be the Lord of my life, and if You say I have to forgive, then I'll do it, if for no other reason than just out of respect and obedience to You."

"So right now, I forgive..." and I called his name. I said, "I still feel like killing him, but if I wait until I feel like forgiving him, I know I'll never do it. So I'm just going to obey You and my feelings will have to catch up later. Right now, on..." and I stated the date, "at this time," and I looked at my watch and said the time, "I officially forgive..." and I said his name again.

"The next time thoughts of this situation come into my mind, I'm going to say out loud, 'Nope, he's forgiven. I forgave him for that.' If the devil himself tries to get me angry over it all, I'm going to have to say, 'I'm sorry, Mr. Devil, but I can't help you. I already forgave him.' And Lord, as for these feelings of anger and rage, I give them to You. I don't want to carry those around with me anymore, and if I do pick them up again, I'm going to bring them right back to You."

I won't lie to you. It took many years before I could think about that time without those negative thoughts and emotions coming up in me, but in all that time I was still able to get my sins forgiven because I obeyed His Word. But unforgiveness can be persistent. Satan will tempt you with it because he knows if he can get you to fall into his trap, you will be crippled spiritually.

I thought I'd dealt with those feelings once and for all. In fact, even though it took some time, I was somewhat proud of myself for how good of a job I'd done in finally dealing with that. (You see where this is going, right? – Proverbs 16:18). Then a couple of years ago, this same person reached out to me on Facebook in a private message with a sincere apology.

In an instant all those feelings came flooding back. My first thought was, "Yeah, right!" I told my wife, "Guess who just messaged me on Facebook! Can you believe the nerve of this guy?" She just shook her head and smiled, and said to me, "You already know what you're going to have to do." God uses her like that sometimes, where they both gang up on me.

I had to go back to that prayer I'd prayed over 30 years ago and pray it all over again. "Lord, I forgave that sucker, and that's all there is to it. He was forgiven and he is forgiven. If I had to testify in court after giving an oath to tell the truth, and the judge asked me, 'Do you want justice for what this man did to you?', I'd have to answer, 'No, your honor, he's already been forgiven.' In obedience to Your Word, I forgive him, Lord."

Again, it took several weeks for my feelings to catch up to my decision. I'm being totally transparent with you here because I want you to see how determined you have to be to walk in the obedience of forgiveness. Forgiveness is a command. You can do it because it's not dependent on how you feel about it. The only thing you have to do is make a choice: Am I going to obey God's Word or not?

Sins Forgiven And Sins Retained

If anyone ever had a right to walk in unforgiveness after the way He was treated, it was Jesus. Yet He forgave. Once again, Jesus is our finest example. His love walk isn't just an ideal that we should look up to. It's an example He intends for us to follow. We think of Jesus as a healer and a miracle worker, but his message was, "Repent, for the Kingdom of God is at hand."

And when he returned to Capernaum after some days, it was reported that he was at home. And

many were gathered together, so that there was no more room, not even at the door. And he was preaching the word to them. And they came, bringing to him a paralytic carried by four men. And when they could not get near him because of the crowd, they removed the roof above him, and when they had made an opening, they let down the bed on which the paralytic lay. And when Jesus saw their faith, he said to the paralytic, "SON, YOUR SINS ARE FORGIVEN." Now some of the scribes were sitting there, questioning in their hearts, "Why does this man speak like that? He is blaspheming! Who can forgive sins but God alone?" And immediately Jesus, perceiving in his spirit that they thus questioned within themselves, said to them, "Why do you question these things in your hearts? Which is easier, to say to the paralytic, 'YOUR SINS ARE FORGIVEN,' or to say, 'Rise, take up your bed and walk'? But that you may know that the Son of Man HAS AUTHORITY ON EARTH TO FORGIVE SINS"—he said to the paralytic— "I say to you, rise, pick up your bed, and go home." And he rose and immediately picked up his bed and went out before them all, so that they were all amazed and glorified God, saying, "We never saw anything like this!" - Mark 2:1-12

A huge part of Jesus' earthly ministry dealt with the forgiveness of sins. Many believers have heard inspiring sermons based on John 14:12:

Truly, truly, I say to you, whoever believes in

me will also do the works that I do; and greater works than these will he do, because I am going to the Father. - John 14:12

We think of the miracles Jesus did and the healings He performed, and we stretch and strain our faith to believe that we might not only match what He did, but somehow exceed it. Yet how many of us ever think of this passage in terms of His authority to forgive sins? Isn't that included in the works that He did? If Jesus has the power to forgive sins, then so do we! He even told His disciples:

If you forgive the sins of any, they are forgiven them; if you withhold forgiveness from any, it is withheld. - John 20:23

Pause for a moment to consider the awesome responsibility that comes with this power He has given to us. When you forgive, He forgives. There's more to this than just you getting past your hurt feelings. There is a weighty spiritual authority that we've been given: the power to forgive. We can forgive the sins of any person, and God will consider them to be forgiven. *Selah.*

Summary

God's goodness leads us to repentance, and then God commands us to forgive, or face serious consequences if we do not. I don't care what anyone did to you, they're not worth your cutting yourself off from the life of the Father. You can forgive despite how you may feel about the person or persons in question, or what they did to you. It can be as simple as making the choice to obey your Lord's command.

You might pray something along the lines of:

"Now God, I've talked to You about my desires, and I know how faithful You are to take care of me. You've been so good to me. Lord, if there are any sins in my life, or any weights that are slowing me down, show them to me right now."

You will probably already have some things in mind that you need to get cleared up. If not, pause for a moment and allow the Holy Spirit an opportunity to show you some areas in your life you may have overlooked where repentance is required. I guarantee you, if you are humble and sincere, something will come to you. When it does, repent and ask God to forgive you.

"Father, I don't want anything to come between You and Me. Any sin, anything inappropriate or displeasing to You, please show it to me now."

Once you've gone through everything that's in your heart, move on to forgive those who have sinned against you.

"Lord, I forgive everybody. I don't want my prayers hindered. I don't want to be blocked from getting forgiveness from You when I need it, so if there's anyone I have anything against in my heart, please show them to me right now so I can forgive them."

Take 10 minutes now to pray through this section of the prayer blueprint. Make sure your heart is free and clear from sin and unforgiveness, so you won't be weighed down. You'll want to be sure that you enter the next phase of your prayer without any condemnation on your conscience.

Chapter 8 Discussion Questions

1. How does beginning prayer with your focus on the Lord make you more susceptible to repentance?

2. When we come before God, does He have a list of our sins in His hand that we need to clear up first? Who is it that keeps a log of the sin in your life?

3. Repentance literally means "to turn around 180 degrees and change direction." Can we repent more than once for the same sin? Why? What would be different from repenting for a sin the first time vs. repenting for that sin the tenth time?

4. Why is it necessary to *confess* our sins to an all-knowing, all-seeing God?

5. You may encounter people who are unaware, unconcerned or unrepentant that they have offended you. What are some temptations you may need to overcome to forgive them?

6. We are commanded to forgive others of the sins they commit against us, but are we commanded to forget? If someone has destroyed our trust, how can we guard our hearts around that person while at the same time being obedient to God's command to forgive?

Chapter 9

Protection Prayers
Your Spiritual Defense

"And lead us not into temptation, but deliver us from evil..." - Matthew 6:13a

The story of redemption is a story of victory over the powers of sin, death and Hell. It's the story of our Father, Who loved us; Who sent His Champion for us; and Who rescued us from the kingdom of darkness and translated us into the kingdom of His dear Son (Colossians 1:13).

Having spent the last phase of your prayer time cleansing yourself by seeking forgiveness and granting forgiveness to others, you are now ready to engage in spiritual warfare. It's time to join your Lord, to stand at His side and to carry out your assignment by doing your part to enforce the victory He paid for so dearly with His own precious Blood.

The thief comes only to steal and kill and destroy. I came that they may have life and have it abundantly. - John 10:10

The players are clearly identified in the Word of God. Satan, the thief, comes only to steal, kill, and destroy.

Jesus came that we might have life, and not just a little bit, but that we might have an abundance of life. In His death, burial and resurrection, Jesus defeated Satan entirely.

Having disarmed principalities and powers, He made a public spectacle of them, triumphing over them in it. - Colossians 2:15 (NKJ)

Jesus is the victorious King. The first thing to understand about spiritual warfare is that the war is over. We share in the victory, but the battle was the Lord's, and He won it all.

I am He who lives, and was dead, and behold, I am alive forevermore. Amen. And I have the keys of Hades and of Death.
- Revelation 1:18 (NKJ)

King Jesus has already accomplished the victory. The enemy remains for a while longer in order to allow us time to rescue more souls from Hell, which was originally intended for Satan and his evil spirits, and was never meant to be a place where people would go (Matthew 25:41).

We are an army of occupation, ever increasing the realm of God's kingdom, ever encroaching on the enemy's territory, ever enforcing His victory. We are occupying until He returns (Luke 19:13).

Resisting Temptation

Satan understands the authority you've been given

in Jesus' name. He knows your potential to harm his interests, even if you don't yet fully realize it. The devil also knows that if he can get you tangled up in sin, you'll be separated from the life of the Father and you won't be able to do him any harm.

With the Spirit of God living inside of you, he recognizes you as a clear and present danger that threatens everything he's worked to accomplish. That's why you've just spent the last portion of your prayer blueprint getting clean from any sin that was sticking to you, and that's why now you're going to pray that you stay clean.

It's not a sin to be tempted. If it were, then Jesus was a sinner, because even He was tempted:

Then Jesus was led up by the Spirit into the wilderness to be tempted by the devil.
  - Matthew 4:1

The question is, what do you do with the temptation when it comes? Temptations usually come in the form of a thought. You have the choice of casting that thought aside or entertaining it. Rev. Kenneth E. Hagin put it this way: "You can't keep the birds from flying over your head, but you can keep them from building a nest in your hair!"

The devil is so low that he'll put a tempting thought into your head, and then as you're thinking about it he'll say to you, "How can you be thinking a thought like that? And you call yourself a Christian!" when he's the one who put the thought there in the first place! He tempts you, and then he tries to condemn you for being tempted.

Tempting thoughts will come. When they do, what will you do with them? That is the issue. You can take comfort in the fact that Jesus was tempted in all the ways you are, yet He was without sin (Hebrews 4:15). That means He understands what you're going through. He knows what it feels like.

The Bible also says that no temptation that comes to you is special or unique. Satan will try to shame you by making you think that no one has ever faced the temptations you're facing, but that isn't true:

No temptation has overtaken you that is not common to man. God is faithful, and he will not let you be tempted beyond your ability, but with the temptation he will also provide the way of escape, that you may be able to endure it. - I Corinthians 10:13

Not only will God not allow you to be overwhelmed with temptations that are too big for you to endure, but He will always provide a way for you to get away from that temptation. When you experience temptation, always look for the way of escape.

I remember one time I was on my computer late at night, in my home office in the basement. My wife and kids were on the second floor and had been asleep for hours. As I sat there working on whatever it was I was doing, an email came in. It was one of those spam emails you get from time to time, and this particular one was promoting a pornographic website.

I'm not going to lie to you. It was late at night. Everyone else in the house was fast asleep. I was tempted to click on that email. The thoughts were rolling through my head, "Go ahead and click on it, who will ever know? Just take a quick look and see what it's about. Satisfy your curiosity, then you can close it and forget about it."

Temptation is like coming to a fork in the road, where one direction is the right way and the other is the wrong way. You haven't sinned until you actually start moving down the wrong path. However, the more you think about it, the longer you let that temptation linger, the more likely you'll be to slip into it and start down that wrong path.

I know you all want to know what happened next, so let me get to it. As my finger hovered over the mouse button, I felt a presence in the room, standing on the basement stairs. I looked over, and while I couldn't see anything with my natural eyes, in the spirit I saw a tall, dark shadowy figure. I immediately recognized this as the spiritual gift of the discerning of spirits (I Corinthians 12:10). This creature was just standing there on the staircase, quietly watching me.

I started to pray, "Lord, why are you showing me this? That thing over there, what is he doing?" The Spirit answered me, *"He's waiting to see whether he's going to be allowed to touch you."* I thought, "Touch me? That's weird. How does he think he's going to do that?" As I tried to grasp what the Spirit was telling me, this scripture came to my mind:

We know that whoever is born of God does not

sin; but he who has been born of God keeps himself, and the wicked one does not touch him. - I John 5:18

"He's watching you to see what you do next," the Holy Spirit told me. *"He wants to touch your finances, your health, and your ministry. If you give in to this temptation, then he will have the right to touch your life."*

All of a sudden clicking on that spam email didn't seem so attractive anymore! I wondered for a moment whether Jesus had ever dealt with temptations like this one, then I remembered Hebrews 4:15 and I realized that He must have. I intend no disrespect, God knows my heart, but it was a comfort to me to know that Jesus had faced similar temptations and overcame them.

I also remembered to look for a way of escape out of this temptation, which in this case was pretty simple. Instead of opening the email, I highlighted it and clicked delete. Then I thanked God for His mercy and grace. I'm not ashamed to tell you this story because it isn't a sin to be tempted. Satan will try to make you think temptation and sin are the same, but remember that even Jesus was tempted.

Sometimes you will struggle with temptation in the flesh, and your mind will come up with all kinds of rationalizations to justify it, but the temptation itself isn't a sin and neither is the mental struggle you experience while you're trying to decide what you're going to do next.

Temptation is going to state its case, and its

presentation is often very convincing. However, sin has been committed only when you decide to give in to the temptation and not before. By definition, no sin can be committed until you commit to it.

Sometimes temptation can be very strong and the way of escape isn't so clear. Jesus didn't tell us to pray, "And lead us not into temptation, but deliver us from evil..." for no reason. There are occasions when you'll have to endure temptation, sometimes for extended periods of time. To learn how to do that, we need to look to our example once again, the Lord Jesus Christ.

Spiritual Warfare

Many Christians are familiar with the Apostle Paul's writings regarding the armor of God in Ephesians 6:10-18. If you've never read about that before, take a moment now to review this passage. Paul, inspired by the Holy Spirit, tells us to put on the whole armor of God. But did you know that someone else wore that armor before we did?

He put on righteousness as a breastplate,
  and a helmet of salvation on his head;
he put on garments of vengeance for clothing,
  and wrapped himself in zeal as a cloak.
  - Isaiah 59:17

This verse is part of a prophecy about the Redeemer who would come, the Lord Jesus Christ. We don't go into battle against the devil wearing just any old random armor. We come against him wearing the armor of the Lord Himself. Also note how Paul's "armor of God" teaching ends:

And take the helmet of salvation, and the sword of the Spirit, which is the word of God, praying at all times in the Spirit, with all prayer and supplication. To that end keep alert with all perseverance, making supplication for all the saints - Ephesians 6:17, 18

This armor of God is prayer armor. It's not physical armor you'd wear to fight a physical opponent. It's spiritual armor. Why does a believer need armor? In fact, if Jesus already won the victory, why do we as believers need to fight at all? The answer is we are here to enforce the spiritual victory that Christ won on our behalf over 2000 years ago.

During World War II the Japanese Empire swept across the south Pacific Ocean, occupying almost every island, even the tiny ones that were of little strategic value. They fortified all of these islands heavily with concrete bunkers and pillboxes, and even tunnels on some islands connecting their various defensive positions.

Capturing these heavily defended islands would have resulted in an average of 3-5 dead Allied soldiers for every Japanese soldier killed, so the Allies made a strategic decision. They attacked only the larger islands, the ones that were big enough to have airstrips built on them, and they bypassed all of the smaller islands.

As the Allied navies gradually took control of the seas, enemy soldiers on these smaller islands were not able to be resupplied. Finally, American bombers were able to reach the Japanese home islands, and the war in the Pacific theater ended. After the Japanese surrendered, victorious

American forces occupied Japan. Yet, there were still many isolated pockets of Japanese forces who were cut off from their command and therefore didn't know the war had ended.

Allied occupation forces reached these pockets of enemy troops one by one, letting them know that the war was over so they could return home with honor. They also freed the people whose islands had been occupied. Sometimes the Japanese soldiers fought back, not believing the Emperor had surrendered and thinking the Allies were trying to trick them. In extreme cases, family members from Japan were transported onto the scene to convince them it was true.

The war in the Pacific had been over since August 15, 1945, yet the victory had to be enforced by the occupying armies. The last Imperial Japanese soldier to surrender, Lt. Hiroo Onoda, fought on for another 29 years, before finally coming in from the jungles of the Philippines on March 19, 1972! This history is a helpful illustration of what we as Christians face today.

Jesus won the victory over Satan and the kingdom of darkness over 2000 years ago, but we must enforce that victory through spiritual occupation in every area of life. In doing so, we extend the boundaries of the Kingdom of Heaven, occupying until He comes. Unlike the Allies in World War II, we're not occupying physical lands. The territory we occupy are the souls of men.

Just as saved families lead to saved households, saved peoples lead to saved nations. The spoils of war are far more precious than lands or material goods. We occupy and enforce His victory in order to gain as many eternal spirits for His Kingdom as we can. I don't know about you, but I decided a long time ago that I'm going to run to the land of the living, and take everyone that I can with me.

Deliverance From Evil

So, if we are working to expand the borders of the Kingdom by filling it with the eternal souls of men, who are our opposing forces? The Bible tells us very clearly in that same passage from Ephesians:

> **Finally, be strong in the Lord and in the strength of his might. Put on the whole armor of God, that you may be able to stand against the schemes of the devil. FOR WE DO NOT WRESTLE AGAINST FLESH AND BLOOD, but against the rulers, against the authorities, against the cosmic powers over this present darkness, against the spiritual forces of evil in the heavenly places.**
> **- Ephesians 6:10-12**

Our enemies are Satan with his fallen angels and demons, who still have reign where men will allow them to, despite Christ's victory in the cross and the resurrection. Many Christians wonder why this is so, and why God allows a defeated Satan to continue to be active in the Earth.

Could God shut them down, send them to Hell, and bring this thing to a close right now? He could, but then all of those people still trapped in the kingdom of darkness would go to Hell with them.

Jesus said Hell was created for the devil and his angels (Matthew 25:41). It was never intended that any human spirit should go there. So for their sake, in the hopes that they might be won to His Kingdom, our Lord delays His return for a little longer.

We need to let them know, just like those Japanese soldiers had to be told, that the war is over. God through Christ has reconciled the world to Himself (II Corinthians 5:19). The debt owed for sin has been paid, the justice demanded by God's holiness has been satisfied, and they were saved over 2000 years ago if only they knew it. Let's tell them!

However, there is resistance to our occupying force, and I don't mean atheists, or Muslims, or other people with religious beliefs that oppose Christianity. No, I'm talking about the ones who are behind those people, pulling their strings like puppets:

For though we walk in the flesh, we are not waging war according to the flesh. For the weapons of our warfare are not of the flesh but have divine power to destroy strongholds.
- II Corinthians 10:3, 4

We, the occupying army of the Church, are not engaging a physical enemy. Our opponents are evil spirits, and they have to be subdued through the power of prayer. Don't ever think that just because you're meeting resistance, that means you're outside of the will of God. If you know you're outside of the will of God and you're getting hammered by the enemy because of it, that's one thing. Just repent and get back in His will.

Yet many times we'll be doing everything right, reading the Bible and praying regularly, walking in love, and allowing the Lord to minister to the people around us through our lives, and that's when we get hit. It's because what you're doing is a threat to the enemy, and he will attempt to create circumstances to hinder you.

Hindering you is all he can do, though. He can't stop you. If you are faithful and you stick to the Word, you will always come out on top in the end, and the enemy's kingdom will shrink even further. Satan cannot win because he's already lost. Jesus spoiled his kingdom and made a public spectacle of him in front of all of his demons (Colossians 2:15).

Isn't that what Jesus did when Satan tempted him in the wilderness? Jesus used the Word of God to fight the devil off (Matthew 4:1-11). That's why it's so important to remember that the second step to the prayer of petition is to make sure you find Bible verses that cover the things you're praying for (see Appendix B on page 178).

Understanding this truth can also help you when you're having trouble with forgiveness. The next time someone is coming against you and acting crazy, recognize that it's not them so much as the spirit behind them who's motivating them to act that way. Yes, people do have to yield to evil spirits to be used by them that way, but usually they don't realize that's what they're doing.

You can come against that evil spirit in prayer, while

at the same time you can love that person, taking pity on them for the bondage they're in as you work to set them free. Jesus said:

Truly, I say to you, whatever you bind on earth shall be bound in heaven, and whatever you loose on earth shall be loosed in heaven.
   - Matthew 18:18

We have the authority to bind evil spirits in the name of Jesus. When we do, then we can take away their treasure by freeing the imprisoned souls of men.

Or how can someone enter a strong man's house and plunder his goods, unless he first binds the strong man? Then indeed he may plunder his house. - Matthew 12:29

Finally, you need to know that you can pray a hedge of protection around yourself and your family. Job had a hedge of protection around himself, and the enemy couldn't touch him. The devil complained to God:

Have you not put a hedge around him and his house and all that he has, on every side? You have blessed the work of his hands, and his possessions have increased in the land.
   - Job 1:10

How would you like that kind of defense system protecting your life? As with everything else in the Christian life, you already have it. Psalm 91 makes an excellent prayer of protection. This is a prayer for

Christians only. Non-Christians can't pray this prayer, since the basis of the protection is revealed in verse 14:

> **Because he holds fast to me in love, I will deliver him; I will protect him, because he knows my name. - Psalms 91:14**

Thank God we're not at the mercy of the devil any longer. We can speak the Word against him, we can bind him in Jesus' name, and we can pray a hedge of protection about ourselves so he can't touch us. What a blessing to be able to pray, "deliver us from evil."

Summary

We have arrived at the fifth section of Jesus' prayer blueprint, having prayed the following thus far:

1) Our Father which art in heaven, Hallowed be thy name.
2) Thy kingdom come. Thy will be done in earth, as it is in heaven.
3) Give us this day our daily bread.
4) And forgive us our debts, as we forgive our debtors.

Now we add, *"and lead us not into temptation, but deliver us from evil."* This is a vitally important section of your prayer session. The enemy will come against you. He will try to oppose everything you're trying to do with the Lord, so you must resist him.

Pray that God will help you to resist temptation so you don't open a door to let the enemy in, and pray that

God will protect you from the attacks of the enemy that come even when you haven't left any doors open for him. Take 10 minutes right now to pray along these lines:

"Heavenly Father, I ask that You help me resist temptation and always do what's right. I thank You that You always make a way of escape when I'm tempted. Help me to see that way of escape and give me the strength to take it when You reveal it to me.

"Father, the enemy is trying to come against me and my family but I bind him right now in the name of Jesus. He will not stir up strife in my marriage, nor will he torment my children. He might oppose me, but he cannot win because Jesus already won. The victory is mine, and the battle is Yours."

Continue to bind Satan in whatever other areas of your life you discern to be under attack: health, finances, relationships, your job, your ministry, or your possessions (car, home, etc.)

"Heavenly Father, I ask You to place a hedge of protection around me. Hide me from the enemy, familiar spirits, and all demon spirits, making it difficult, if not impossible for them to effectively track or trace me in the realm of the spirit.

"There shall be no penetrations of this hedge of protection, according to Your Word in Psalm 91. I know that You will answer this prayer because I love You and I trust in Your name only. I pray that the Blood of the Lord Jesus Christ will cover me and all that You have given me, and

that the enemy will not have access to what has been given to me. Thank You for Your divine protection in Jesus Name, Amen."

As always, pray in your own words, expanding this example prayer as needed. Now, with the enemy's evil designs taken care of for the moment, you're ready to end this prayer where you began: with praise to your King.

Chapter 9 Discussion Questions

1. Are temptation and committing sin the same? Is it a sin to be tempted? Why or why not?

2. How does understanding the difference between being tempted vs. committing sin help us resist temptation?

3. We face a defeated foe (Satan) and a disarmed kingdom of darkness. What does this reveal about your capacity to overcome temptation?

4. "The enemy remains for a while longer in order to allow us time to rescue more souls from Hell." What impact might our ability to overcome temptation have upon the unsaved people we're praying for?

5. When you are tempted, you will never go through anything that others have not also been through (I Corinthians 10:13). Why should we be encouraged by this knowledge?

6. How did Jesus resist temptation? What are some things you can do to resist temptation? What habits do you have to keep yourself strong? How might you avoid future temptations?

Chapter 10

Declaration Prayers
Enforcing the Victory

"For yours is the kingdom and the power and the glory forever. Amen." - Matthew 6:13b (NKJ)

So far we've entered into the Father's presence, focusing on Him and the greatness of His names. We've prayed that the authority of His Kingdom would reign in our lives, and that everything would be done according to His will.

Then we shifted the focus to ourselves, bringing our personal needs and desires to Him in prayer, standing on the promises of His holy written Word. Next we sought repentance as necessary and granted forgiveness in obedience to His command. Finally, we prayed for protection from temptation and the attacks of the enemy who tries to resist our spiritual progress.

Now we finish where we began, with the focus moving off of the needs of our own life and back to the greatness of our Heavenly Father. We do this by making three very simple, yet very profound, faith declarations.

For Yours Is The Kingdom

Why did you work your way through the first five sections of this prayer pattern? Why are you even praying in the first place? For what? "For Yours is the Kingdom."

You're doing this for the Kingdom of God. That's why this book is in your hands. That's why you're putting forth the effort to find out what it will take for you to be able to enjoy a more consistent prayer life. For the Kingdom. But what makes the Kingdom so special?

The Kingdom is special because of the One to Whom it belongs. It's His Kingdom, the Kingdom of God. This is the inspiration that must motivate your prayer life. Let it be your touchstone. Let it be the fire from Heaven that consumes you.

The kingdoms of the world have become the kingdom of our Lord and of his Christ, and he shall reign forever and ever. – Revelation 11:15

You're not fulfilling a religious obligation. You're not just going through the motions so you can mark off a box on a checklist, or impress your fellow believers — not if you're smart. No, you're doing all of this intentionally, for a purpose. You're doing it for something and for Someone.

When I ask myself, "Why have I decided to make prayer a priority?" The answer is, "I'm doing it for You, My Lord, and for Your Kingdom. I recognize the awesome power of prayer, as well as the sublime privilege of prayer, but in the final analysis it's not about me. It's about You.

It's all about You, and it always has been. For Yours is the Kingdom."

Willpower alone is not sufficient to maintain a consistent prayer life. It isn't even enough to want to be a good Christian. There's absolutely nothing inside of yourself that's capable of achieving the kind of prayer life your heart yearns for, not in your own ability. Without Him you can do nothing (John 15:5). Yet with Him all things are possible (Matthew 19:26).

Such is the confidence that we have through Christ toward God. Not that we are sufficient in ourselves to claim anything as coming from us, but our sufficiency is from God.
- II Corinthians 3:4-5

When you pray, "For Yours is the Kingdom," you are acknowledging God's possession of His Kingdom, and also His position as the King. By reminding yourself of Who you're doing this for, and Who He is, your King, you're also reminding yourself of the source of your spiritual power and of your total reliance on Him.

And The Power

Not only is the Kingdom His, but so is the power. We hear a lot about the power of God, but it seems that too often the emphasis is on the word "power" instead of the word "God." Everyone wants the power, but not everyone wants to get close enough to Him to get it. Yet, if you have Him, you automatically have His power.

And I, when I came to you, brothers, did not come proclaiming to you the testimony of God with lofty speech or wisdom. For I decided to know nothing among you except Jesus Christ and him crucified. And I was with you in weakness and in fear and much trembling, and my speech and my message were not in plausible words of wisdom, but in demonstration of the Spirit and of POWER, so that your faith might not rest in the wisdom of men but in the POWER of God.
- I Corinthians 2:1-5

The Apostle Paul was a highly educated man, yet when he ministered he didn't rely on those credentials. Instead, he demonstrated the Word to his audience with the power of the Holy Spirit. In other words, he let the miracles do the talking for him. Paul understood the prayer, *"Yours is the power."*

For I am not ashamed of the gospel, for it is the power of God for salvation to everyone who believes, to the Jew first and also to the Greek.
- Romans 1:16

Paul preached that the Gospel is the power of God. The Greek word used for power in both of these verses is *dunamis*. We get our English word "dynamite" from this word, so many people assume *dunamis* simply describes the explosive power of God, similar to the way dynamite explodes. However, that's not what it actually means.

Dunamis is defined not only as "strength, power, and

ability," but also as "inherent power, power residing in a thing by virtue of its nature." In other words, the Word of God in the message of the Gospel contains within itself the power to bring itself to pass. Just like the full potential of the oak tree is contained in an acorn, so the dunamis of God is contained within His Word.

Trust in the Lord with all your heart,
  and do not lean on your own understanding.
In all your ways acknowledge him,
  and he will make straight your paths.
    - Proverbs 3:5, 6

When we declare that the power is all God's, we're simultaneously admitting that the power is not our own. The Bible is full of warnings about not trying to do spiritual things in our own strength. In fact, trusting in our own strength will ultimately cause us to turn away from Him.

Thus says the Lord:
"Cursed is the man who trusts in man
  and makes flesh his strength,
  whose heart turns away from the Lord."
    - Jeremiah 17:5

Instead of relying on our own strength, we must rely on His power, and that's especially true when it comes to prayer. You cannot maintain a consistent prayer life in your own strength, but thank God prayer isn't something you do by yourself for God, but rather something you do together with Him.

> **Then he said to me, "This is the word of the Lord to Zerubbabel: Not by might, nor by power, but by my Spirit, says the Lord of hosts.**
> **- Zechariah 4:6**

When we pray, *"Yours is the power,"* we are acknowledging our total dependence on Him. Don't ever try to walk in the power of the flesh and your own understanding. Rely on the anointing of the Holy Spirit. Learn to look to Him.

When I was a young Christian in the 1980's, the Lord used to give me prophetic poems. One in particular was about the futility of certain Christians trying to effect change in our nation through political action alone. The last line of that poem has come back to me several times over the years because I've been able to apply it in so many different situations, and it also applies to prayer: *"No anointing, disappointing."*

And The Glory, Forever

Finally, after declaring that His is the Kingdom — recognizing that it's not about you, but all about Him, and after declaring that His is the power — acknowledging that we are powerless in ourselves to bring about the changes that we need, we close by declaring that His is the glory, forever.

We need to understand our purpose and why we were made in the first place. You were created to glorify God, and to worship Him forever. What does it mean to give God the glory? That's a phrase we hear thrown around a lot, but what does it really mean? Glory is defined as: "public praise, honor, or distinction extended by common consent."

In keeping with the theme that it's all about Him, we close our prayer blueprint by agreeing to give God all of the credit. Not some of the glory, not most of the glory, but all of the glory. John the Baptist understood this:

He must increase, but I must decrease.
- John 3:30

Once we've acknowledged that His is the Kingdom and His is the power, it's very easy to also recognize that He alone is worthy to receive the glory. As a Christian, what you must understand is that your life will continuously improve when you walk in obedience to His Word.

You can be certain that there will be tests and trials along the way, but God will even use those to bring you to a better place by the time they are done. As your life gets better, the people around you, those who are close to you, will begin to notice the change in you.

When that happens, make no mistake, you will be tempted to take the credit for it. Don't ever accept the glory that belongs to God. Yes, you had your part to play. Yes, you were obedient to His Word. Yes, you yielded to His will.

Yet, it's only because of Him that you even had a part to play. Without His Word, there would be nothing for you to obey. Without His plan for your life, there would be nothing for you to yield yourself to. Always give God the glory for every blessing that comes to you.

> **Now to him who is able to do far more abundantly than all that we ask or think, according to the power at work within us, to him be GLORY in the church and in Christ Jesus throughout all generations, forever and ever. Amen. - Ephesians 3:20, 21**

Notice how this prayer of supplication Paul wrote in his letter to the Ephesians (3:14-21) ends in exactly the same way as the prayer pattern Jesus gave us. Just as in Jesus' teaching, two thoughts are emphasized here at the end by Paul: to God be the glory, and it's forever.

As Christians, we need to make an effort to maintain our eternal perspective. You are an eternal being who's going to exist forever, and while it may be hard to wrap your finite mind around it now, God's Word assures us that in Heaven we will be joyously happy throughout eternity.

However, Satan will attempt to distract you from the truth of your eternal destiny. Through temptation and the manipulation of circumstances against you, he will try to get your mind to focus on the moment instead of forever. He knows that if he can get you to live only in the moment, he'll be able to make your impact on eternity much less effective.

King David once made the mistake of getting caught up in the moment. Standing on the roof of his palace, when he should have been out with his army, he allowed temptation to overtake him when he spied on Bathsheba bathing on the roof of her house below him.

II Samuel chapters 11 and 12 tell the story of how David seduced her and accidentally got her pregnant. Then he tried to deceive her husband, Uriah, into thinking the child was his. When that didn't work, David had Uriah killed so that he could take Bathsheba for himself. God was unhappy, and publicly revealed David's sin through His prophet, Nathan.

As part of God's judgment on David for his sin, Nathan declared that their baby would die. Shortly after the child was born, he became very sick. David fasted and prayed for the child to live, but to no avail. It wasn't long until the child was dead, and although the servants of David's household were afraid to tell him, David figured it out.

What happened next was very odd. The Israelites were a very outwardly expressive people. When they were happy, they were really happy and they partied hard. When they were sad, they were really sad. They wept aloud, tore their clothes, and kneeled on the ground and threw dirt in their hair. It wasn't unusual for mourning to continue for days or even weeks.

Yet when David understood that Bathsheba's child had died, he simply stood, cleaned himself up, and went to the house of the Lord to worship. It was such an unusual reaction, and so uncharacteristic of their culture, that the servants had to ask David, "Why aren't you any more upset than you are?"

He said, "While the child was still alive, I fasted
and wept, for I said, 'Who knows whether the
Lord will be gracious to me, that the child may
live?' But now he is dead. Why should I fast? Can
I bring him back again? I shall go to him, but he
will not return to me." - II Samuel 12:22, 23

While leaning on the power of his own strength,
David got caught up in the moment and yielded to
temptation, but now he had learned his lesson. He told his
servants, "The baby isn't coming back now, but one day I'll
go where he is and I'll get to see him again." David had
successfully recovered his eternal perspective.

This popular story from the Old Testament reveals
a great truth: maintaining an eternal perspective will help
you to live "in the moment" in a way that will still be
pleasing to God. When we pray, *"For yours is the Kingdom,
and the power, and the glory... forever,"* we are realigning
our perspective, not just off of ourselves and onto Him, but
also out of the transitory realm and into the eternal.

Summary

The prayer blueprint Jesus gave to us, His disciples,
concludes with the word, "Amen." Amen doesn't mean,
"The End – the prayer is over now." It literally translates as
"let it be," or "so be it." In other words, everything that I've
prayed for the last hour, through all six sections of Jesus'
prayer pattern, may all of it come to pass just as I've
believed. So be it.

Just as you've done at the end of each section of the

prayer outline so far, take about 10 minutes to pray through this last part now.

"Father God, I pray this prayer not for me, but for You, because it's not about me, but it's all about You. Yours is the Kingdom. It is an expanding kingdom, and I am a part of Your spiritual army, occupying until You come.

"Give me the strength and the courage to declare that the kingdoms of the world have become the Kingdom of my Lord and of His Christ, and He shall reign forever and ever.

"Father God, Yours is also the power. I rely on you alone. I lean on the Holy Spirit and His anointing. I don't trust in the arm of the flesh, or in my own understanding. I put my faith in Your power, because You are well able to bring your promises to pass. I thank you that the Gospel is Your power unto salvation.

"Finally, Lord, the glory is Yours alone. You get all of the credit. Everything I've learned, everything I've done, everything I am, ALL of the glory goes to You. Don't ever let me take credit for the things that You have done. I must decrease and You must increase.

"In Jesus' mighty Name,
Amen."

Chapter 10 Discussion Questions

1. Why does Matthew 6:13 read, "For yours is THE kingdom and THE power and THE glory forever..." as opposed to, "For yours is A kingdom and A power and A glory forever..."?

2. America has "citizens," but monarchies like the United Kingdom have "subjects." How does viewing yourself as a subject of the King help your prayer life?

3. Why should you maintain a constant awareness of your divine citizenship? Referring back to chapters 1 through 9, what are some of the rights of a citizen in the Father's Kingdom?

4. Many people wish for things to change or hope that good things will happen. What is the fundamental difference between wishing and praying?

5. Young cooks will often follow a recipe precisely, but experienced chefs know what to add to make the food taste the best. How did they get this knowledge? From a book? How is learning to cook similar to learning how to pray?

6. When you turn on a light switch you can see the power of electricity. What does the power of God look like? What evidence of that power do you have in your life?

7. How will keeping your eternal perspective change how you view your life? This world? Eternity?

Conclusion

After this manner therefore pray ye:
Our Father which art in heaven,
Hallowed be thy name.
Thy kingdom come, Thy will be done
in earth, as it is in heaven.
Give us this day our daily bread.
And forgive us our debts, as we forgive our debtors.
And lead us not into temptation, but deliver us from evil:
For thine is the kingdom, and the power,
and the glory, for ever. Amen.
- Matthew 6:9-13 (KJV)

As you've read through the chapters of this book, if you've taken the time to pray for ten minutes through each of these six sections of Jesus' prayer outline, let me be the first to congratulate you: you've just prayed for one hour!

Now, if the thought of praying for an entire hour is still a little overwhelming to you, don't be discouraged. Instead of praying through this prayer blueprint for ten minutes each section, just pray for five minutes per section. You'll still be praying for 30 minutes every day, and that's a lot, especially if you started out at zero minutes per day.

The key is consistency. Every year people who have spent the holidays from Thanksgiving through the end of

December stuffing themselves full of food realize they need to lose some weight. They make a New Year's resolution to join a gym, and they start off strong, going every day and working out for 3-4 hours at a time.

Soon they drop off, and before long they aren't going to the gym at all because they set unrealistic expectations for themselves that no one could live up to. It would have been much better for them if they'd gone to the gym for just 30 minutes, every other day, and done so consistently. Instead, they set themselves up to fail.

People make the same mistake when it comes to exercising spiritually. They'll read a book like this, get all inspired and excited, and then try to read their Bible for four hours a day and pray for another four hours. Don't do that. You would be so much better off if you would just read one or two chapters from the Bible and then pray for 30 minutes a day, yet do it consistently every day.

I can tell you what will happen when you do this: your prayer life will move from discipline to desire, and you will come to look forward to your daily calls with your King. It won't be long before 5 minutes per section just won't be enough. You'll have too much to say!

And remember, prayer is a conversation, not a monologue. Take a moment during each part of your prayer session to pause and allow the Holy Spirit to speak to your heart. He's been sent to help you (John 14:16), and that includes helping you in prayer. Don't be that guy who always monopolizes the conversation. Give Him a chance to talk as well.

As you grow in prayer, you'll learn much more about it, but you have more than enough right here to get you started. There's so much more that could be said on this subject. I could write 100 books like this one and never even scratch the surface. Just remember that learning to pray is a lot like when you learned how to drive: you learn best by actually doing it.

You have the outline now, straight from the mouth of Jesus. You need to begin praying every day, using Jesus' prayer blueprint as your pattern. The only thing left for you to do is take action.

I'm so excited for you, because it's now time for you to truly begin experiencing real progress toward real power, now that you know *How To Pray*.

Closing Prayer

Heavenly Father, I thank You for the grace you've given me to write this book. I pray that I've been able to bring it forth to the readers as You want it brought forth, emphasizing the things that You want emphasized. I ask that any mistakes or errors on my part would be overshadowed by the teaching ministry of the Holy Spirit for the readers.

For those who have read How To Pray, I pray that the revelations they've gained won't be just information and data in their heads, but impartations of truth within their hearts and spirits. I pray You will encourage them as they begin to put their spiritual lives in order so that they become disciplined in the practice of prayer.

I ask that the haphazard and random prayer life they've had up until now will be replaced with consistent, intentional planning sessions with you, Almighty God, prayer sessions in which they will be able to address any desires they have and get clear direction from Heaven.

Finally, dear Father, I pray that all who have read this book will be able to take the skills they've learned and use them to thoroughly enjoy the time they get to spend together with You.

In the mighty Name of the Lord Jesus Christ I pray.

Amen.

Appendix A

And he came to the disciples and found them sleeping. And he said to Peter, "So, could you not watch with me one hour?" - Matthew 26:40

This outline is based on the prayer blueprint Jesus taught in Matthew 6:9-13 and Luke 11:2-4. Spend just 10 minutes praying on each section of the prayer and you will have prayed for one hour. Pray through this outline daily for your spiritual growth.

Our Father in heaven, Hallowed be Your name.
Section I - Position & Promises (10 minutes)

PRAISE

Acknowledge God as your Father
- Thank Him that you've been adopted into the Father's family
- Thank Him for the shed Blood of Jesus that made your redemption possible

Acknowledge God is a good Father
- Thank Him for all the ways He's blessed you (thanksgiving)
- Thank Him for hearing your prayer (faith)

Acknowledge that He is in Heaven
- Recognize His superior position (humility)
- Recognize His superior perspective (trust)

WORSHIP

Hallow His Name
- Thank God for the power that is in the Name of Jesus
- Worship God as Jehovah - I AM
- Thank God that He is whatever you need Him to be

Worship God with the Names He uses to reveal Himself

Redemptive Name:	Associated Benefit:
Jehovah-Tsidkenu	Righteousness & Forgiveness
Jehovah-Shalom	Peace
Jehovah-Rapha	Healing
Jehovah-Jireh	Provision
Jehovah-Sabaoth	Protection
Jehovah-Nissi	Unity
Jehovah-M'Kaddesh	Sanctification
Jehovah-Shammah	Indwelling Holy Spirit
Jehovah-Rohi	Guidance and Direction

Your kingdom come.
Your will be done on earth as it is in heaven.
Section II - Priorities (10 minutes)

First pray for national leaders, then state and local leaders
- Pray for peaceful conditions ideal for the spreading of the Gospel
- Pray for the peace of Jerusalem
- Pray for the spiritual harvest of souls to come in

Next pray for God's Kingdom to come in your own life
- Take authority over every sphere of life where you have influence
- Pray for your spouse, your children and other family members
- Pray for your job, your employer, and co-workers

Then pray for your local church
- Pray for your Pastor
- Pray for wisdom for church leaders
- Pray for faithfulness in the congregation

Pray God's will be done on Earth as in Heaven
- Take authority over any circumstances opposed to God's Word
- Thank God that the Holy Spirit has been sent to help you
- Pray for clarity of direction in life and ministry

Give us this day our daily bread.
Section III - Provision (10 minutes)

Pray through any new petitions that you have added to your prayer journal
- Decide on exactly what you want
- Find Scriptures which cover the subject (see page 178)
- Ask for what you desire
- Believe that you receive
- Thank God for the answer

Review your Prayer Journal and Thank God for all of the...
- Answered prayers that have already manifested in your life
- Things you've believed you've received and are still standing in faith for

Ask God to reveal to you if there's anything else you should ask for

And forgive us our debts,
As we forgive our debtors.
Section IV - People (10 minutes)

Ask God to reveal to you any sin in your life
- Truly repent for whatever He shows you
- Ask God to help you make better choices in the future

Ask God to reveal to you any spiritual weights in your life
- Let God show you how they are slowing you down spiritually
- Pray about how you might deal differently with these areas of your life

Ask God to show you the people in your life whom you need to forgive
- Obey His command to forgive anyone that He shows you
- Release them in the spirit so those sins will no longer be retained against them

And do not lead us into temptation, but deliver us from the evil one.
Section V - Protection & Power (10 minutes)

Overcoming Temptation
- Thank God that He understands your temptations
- Recognize that Christ was tempted in all the same ways you are
- Pray that you will find the way of escape God provides when tempation comes

Spiritual Warfare - Protection
- Ask God to reveal any Satanic assignments against you
- Plead the Blood of Jesus Christ over your life
- Put on the whole armor of God (Ephesians 6:10-18)
- Pray a hedge of protection around your life (Psalms 91)

Spiritual Warfare - Occupation
- Thank God for your spiritual liberation in Christ, and deliverance from the kingdom of darkness
- Recognize that your true enemies are spiritual, not flesh and blood
- Thank God that you have authority over evil spirits in the Name of Jesus
- Bind any devils and loose God's angels in the situations God reveals to you

For Yours is the kingdom and the power and the glory forever. Amen
Section VI - Praise (10 minutes)

The Kingdom
- Recognize your dual-citizenship as a subject of the Kingdom of Heaven, with all of the rights and privileges that come with that status
- Ask God to continue to reveal to you what your role is regarding occupying until He comes

The Power

- Acknowledge the power of God contained within the Gospel
- Recognize your total reliance on Him, and refuse to rely on your own strength or your own understanding
- Ask for grace and the anointing of the Holy Spirit to carry out what He's called you to do

The Glory

- Acknowledge God alone is worthy to receive all of the glory
- Commit to never take God's glory for yourself
- Ask God to reveal to you other areas in your life where He could be glorified

Forever

- Recognize that you are a creature destined for eternity
- Ask God to help you keep your eternal perspective on your life and the circumstances you face
- Pray that you won't be sidetracked by the distractions of the moment

Amen - So Be It

- Praise God for allowing you the privilege of spending time to talk with him
- Praise God for granting you the amazing power of prayer
- Praise God for His faithfulness in answering your prayers

You can download a separate copy of this
One Hour Prayer Outline for yourself at

www.howtoprayguide.com/thankyou

Appendix B

Prayer Scriptures

Here are some scripture lists for some common areas of need that you can use when creating your petition prayers.

These lists are provided to help you get started. They are not comprehensive, so you should feel free to add additional Bible verses that speak to your heart on each subject.

Scriptures for Receiving Healing

Mark 16:18
Proverbs 4:22
Exodus 15:26
Jeremiah 17:14
I Peter 2:24
Isaiah 53:5

Psalms 107:20
Mathew 8:17
Psalms 30:2
Psalms 103:2-3
James 5:14
Jeremiah 30:17

Scriptures for Receiving Peace of Mind

Romans 12:21
Psalms 23:4
Isaiah 54:14
Psalms 91:10-11
Ephesians 6:16
Isaiah 54:13

I John 4:4
Galatians 1:4
Psalms 1:3
Proverbs 12:28
Galatians 3:13
Psalms 119:89

Scriptures for Receiving Material Needs Met

Philippians 4:19
Psalms 23:1
II Corinthians 8:9
Luke 6:38
Proverbs 3:9-10
Joshua 1:8

II Corinthians 9:8
Mathew 6:33
Psalms 119:25
Psalms 37:4
Malahci 3:10
III John 2

Scriptures for Receiving Wisdom

John 16:13
Psalms 119:105
Colossians 3:16
Psalm 107:43
Proverbs 3:5, 6
Job 12:12, 13

I Corinthians 1:30
Romans 12:2
Psalms 138:8
John 10:3-4
Psalm 19:7
James 3:17

Scriptures for Receiving Comfort and Strength

Nehemiah 8:10
Proverbs 4:21, 22
Ephesians 4:15
John 10:28
Ephesians 4:27
Mark 16:17-18

Psalms 27:1
Ephesians 4:29
I John 4:4
Colossians 3:15
Colossians 2:10
Matthew 16:19

Scriptures for Receiving Grace for Meals

Matthew 14:19
Luke 24:30
Deuteronomy 8:10

Matthew 15:36
Acts 27:35
I Timothy 4:4,5

Scripture Index

How Can I Be Saved?

Are you ready to accept the gift of eternal life that Jesus is offering you right now? If you sincerely desire to receive Jesus into your heart as your Lord and Savior, then here's a suggested prayer you can pray. You don't have to use these exact words. What's most important is that you're talking to God from your heart:

> *"Lord Jesus, I know that I am a sinner and I do not deserve eternal life. But, I believe You died and rose from the grave to make me a new creation and to prepare me to dwell in your presence forever. Jesus, come into my life, take control of my life, forgive my sins and save me. I am now placing my trust in You alone for my salvation and I accept your free gift of eternal life."*

Congratulations! You've just been adopted into the family of God. Since the theme of this book is largely focused on the unseen spirit realm, you should be aware of what the angels are doing right now, according to Jesus:

Just so, I tell you, there is joy before the angels of God over one sinner who repents. – Luke 15:10

If you've prayed this prayer for the first time, please contact me at *praisereport@michaeldorseyonline.org* so we can celebrate with you!

About the Author

Saved at the age of 10 and Spirit-filled at age 16, Rev. Michael Dorsey has been a Christian for more than 30 years, and a teacher of the Word of God for over 20 of those years. He has ministered to new believers one-on-one, taught various Bible courses, and has been a speaker at ministers conferences.

Michael is the author of several books, including the multi-volume *How To Live* series. He has been called of God to provide quality outreach materials for true seekers, to build up and strengthen new believers, and to train up mature Christians for more effective service.

His passion is discipling new believers, teaching them the Word of God so they can be transformed from victims into victorious Christians, and then equipping those believers to begin discipling others to the glory of God.

Michael and his wife Katherine, along with their children Robbie and Kirsten, are active partners with Riverside Church in the Baltimore area, where they work in the ministry and assist their Pastor to bless God's people.

THANK YOU!

I hope you've enjoyed this book, *How To Pray - Making Real Progress Toward Real Power*, the second volume in the *How To Live* series. Now you're ready to take your prayer life to the next level of glory in Christ Jesus!

As a personal thank you for reading *How To Pray - Making Real Progress Toward Real Power*, I'd like to invite you to go to ***www.howtoprayguide.com/thankyou***, where you will find additional free resources available for you to download that will further assist you in your daily prayer life.

If you don't yet have your copy of the companion volume to this book, the *How To Pray: Daily Prayer Journal,* I encourage you to order it. Find out more at ***www.howtoprayguide.com/journal***. Once again, thank you so much for your support and your prayers!

Michael Dorsey

How To Pray

Making Real Progress Toward Real Power

is a publication of

*For further information on
the How To Live series,
along with details of other
publications and upcoming projects
designed to equip Christians
to live victoriously,
please visit us at:*

www.malakimpress.com

Made in the USA
Columbia, SC
14 November 2017